MW01124307

Re-Writing International Relations

Global Dialogues: Developing Non-Eurocentric IR and IPE

Series Editors: John M. Hobson, Professor of Politics
and International Relations, University of Sheffield;
L. H. M. Ling, Professor, Milano School of International Affairs,
Management, and Urban Policy, The New School

This series adopts a dialogical perspective on global politics, which focuses on the interactions and reciprocities between West and non-West, across Global North and Global South. Not only do these shape and re-shape each other but they have also shaped, made and remade our international system/global economy for the last 500 years. Acknowledging that these reciprocities may be asymmetrical due to disparities in power and resources, this series also seeks to register how 'Eastern' agency, in tandem with counterparts in the West, has made world politics and the world political economy into what it is. While this series certainly welcomes purely theoretically based books, its primary focus centres on empirical rethinking about the development of the world political system and the global economy along non-Eurocentric lines.

Titles in the Series

Islam and International Relations: Exploring Community and the Limits of Universalism
by Faiz Sheikh

Historical Sociology and World History: Uneven and Combined Development over the Longue Durée, edited by Alexander Anievas and Kamran Matin

Re-Writing International Relations: History and Theory Beyond Eurocentrism in Turkey, by Zeynep Gülşah Çapan

Re-Writing International Relations

History and Theory Beyond Eurocentrism in Turkey

Zeynep Gülşah Çapan

ROWMAN & LITTLEFIELD
INTERNATIONAL

London • New York

Published by Rowman & Littlefield International, Ltd.
Unit A, Whitacre Mews, 26-34 Stannary Street, London SE11 4AB
www.rowmaninternational.com

Rowman & Littlefield International, Ltd. is an affiliate of Rowman & Littlefield
4501 Forbes Boulevard, Suite 200, Lanham, Maryland 20706, USA
With additional offices in Boulder, New York, Toronto (Canada), and Plymouth (UK)
www.rowman.com

British Library Cataloguing in Publication Data
A catalogue record for this book is available from the British Library

ISBN: HB 978-1-7834-8783-7
       PB 978-1-7834-8784-4

Library of Congress Cataloging-in-Publication Data is Available
ISBN 978-1-78348-783-7 (cloth : alk. paper)
ISBN 978-1-78348-784-4 (pbk. : alk. paper)
ISBN 978-1-78348-785-1 (electronic)

♾™ The paper used in this publication meets the minimum requirements of American
National Standard for Information Sciences—Permanence of Paper for Printed Library
Materials, ANSI/NISO Z39.48-1992.

Printed in the United States of America

Contents

Acknowledgements

The writing of this book was a journey and the people I met along the way made it an educational and dare I say an enjoyable one. I want to thank all of them, some of whom I might have forgotten to mention here, for making this journey possible and helping me along the way. Any failings of course remain mine. Firstly, I want to thank Oliver Kessler without whom I would never have been able to write this book. His guidance and kindness have become the standards to which I aspire to. An advice from him still resonates with me which was 'write as if you are explaining it to an eight-year-old'. Leila Khalilova (my niece) had to endure a couple of hours of me explaining my arguments to her because of this advice. After my 'explanation' she looked at me skeptically and said 'It is not really exciting, there are no unicorns'. Alas, I was never able to figure out how to integrate unicorns into the story of international relations but I do hope both Oliver and Leila enjoy the book.

I am not certain any words will be enough to express my gratitude to Ayşe Zarakol who has been an intellectual inspiration, an incredible friend and steadfastly continues to endure my endless ramblings. The writing of the book was made possible by a TUBITAK 2218 post-doctoral grant that allowed me to spend a year at Bilkent University. I want to thank Pınar Bilgin for encouraging me to apply for the post-doctoral grant. Her work constituted one of the starting points for the questions that continue to guide my research and her assistance has been invaluable throughout the process. Lily Ling and John Hobson have been incredibly helpful throughout the process and I want to thank them for their guidance and feedback. I want to also thank Anna Reeve and Dhara Patel for their help throughout the process of publishing the book. The archival material was collected at T. C. Başbakanlık Devlet Arşivleri and Atatürk IBB Kitapliği.

I was lucky enough to teach courses that spoke directly to my area of research both at Marmara University and University of Erfurt. I would like to thank the students who attended the courses and it was through our dialogues, disagreements and discussions that I was able to develop my thinking. Academia can be a lonely existence at times and even alienating. It was thanks to friends I made along the way that it became an environment of inspiration and constant dialogue. Thanks to Senem Aydın-Düzgit, Burç Beşgül, Munevver Cebeci, Filipe Dos Reis, Maj Grasten, Janis Grzybowski, Özge Onursal, Timo Walter and Benjamin Wilhelm. Despite all my efforts, I could not figure out a way to include Niklas Luhmann in the book. The unicorn might have been a more realistic expectation.

A special mention go to my nieces and nephew Sevda, Leila and Iska who made me forget academia when I needed to and let me spend a few hours in their wondrous worlds. Gülüm and Gülben thank you for always being there, there is nothing more comforting in knowing that when all else fails you will always have your sisters. Last but not least I want to thank my mother and father – my mother for her unwavering support and her belief in me even though at times it seemed like and might still seem like I was going after a dream; my father for being the dreamer whom I take after. It is to them that this book is dedicated.

Introduction

The aim of this book is to contribute to discussions about the Eurocentrism of International Relations. The book focuses on the manifestations of Eurocentrism and criticism of Eurocentrism in and through disciplines and geopolitical contexts. *Re-writing International Relations* intervenes in two main debates about the field of IR. The first debate is about the attempts to re-write the history of International Relations,[1] and the second debate is about the Eurocentrism of the field of International Relations.[2] These two debates are interrelated because the way the history of the discipline of International Relations is written constructs the boundaries through which its possible futures can be imagined.

The main focus of the book is the Eurocentrism of the field of International Relations and the question of how to understand it through connecting and thinking in and through disciplinary and geopolitical knowledges. Eurocentrism – how to define and tackle it – has been a concern for the humanities and the social sciences for some time.[3] Eurocentrism and how it manifests, is enacted and circulates is not a uniform story. The aim of the book is to trace how Eurocentrism and its criticisms is expressed in and through disciplinary and geopolitical knowledges. The different manifestations (avatars) of Eurocentrism[4] can be grouped under three headings: culturalist, historical and epistemic.[5] The culturalist avatar refers to the ways in which the East is framed. The historical avatar is about how Europe is taken to be the central subject of history and as the central point from which the main developments of history such as capitalism originated. The epistemic avatar establishes the relationship between the knower and the known.[6] These avatars not only manifest themselves in different and interrelated ways but also evolve and travel and are reproduced and renegotiated.

1

The book intends to trace the possible different manifestations of Eurocentrism and the different criticisms of Eurocentrism. Sanjay Subrahmanyam argues that the aim of connected histories should be to 'redraw maps that emerge from the problematics we wish to study rather than insert problematics to fit our pre-existing categories'.[7] As such, the book contends that rather than problematizing Eurocentrism within the categories through which we work, such as International Relations, the maps that emerge from tracing Eurocentrism need to be focused upon. Thus, the focus of the book is on the maps that emerge out of the problematization of Eurocentrism, whether in tracing its manifestations or the strategies developed to counter it.

STORIES OF INTERNATIONAL RELATIONS

Stories we tell of international relations and of International Relations,[8] as with all stories, serve a purpose, convey a message, construct a past and imagine a future. These stories of international relations and International Relations are not separate but interlinked. What is the story of international relations, and why does it need re-writing? The story of international relations develops in a linear manner whereby the expansion of the international system rests upon an implicit and, at times, explicit reliance on the linear narrative of the 'rise of the West', which has a 'triumphalist teleology':

> with Ancient Greece, progressing on to the European agricultural revolution in the low middle ages, then on to the rise of the Italian-led commerce at the turn of the millennium. The story continues on into the high middle ages when Europe rediscovered pure Greek ideas in the Renaissance which, when coupled with the scientific revolution, the Enlightenment and the rise of democracy, propelled Europe into industrialization and capitalist modernity.[9]

Stories of international relations, international society and International Relations are based upon a story that has Europe at its centre and which edits out the disruptions and constructs a linear unproblematized tale of the 'rise of the West', 'the expansion of International Society' and 'the origins of the state system'. The stories might have different titles – the story of security, the story of the state, the story of the international – and might prioritize different aspects, yet the periodizations, the events and settings are dependent upon a specific understanding of European history.[10]

Both for international relations and for International Relations, these stories are performative.[11] As Waever argues, 'the "debates" operate as a dialectic between implicit pictures and articulate self-representations of the discipline'.[12] Thus, the story of the debates operates to shape 'actual academic practice' and it is also 'constructed and artificially imposed on much more diverse activities'.[13] In that sense, it creates the space within which international relations can be discussed. As such, 'it makes a difference whether one tries to operate in today's IR according to an understanding of this as "after the third debate" or "after the fourth debate"'.[14] The story of IR therefore provides the terrain upon which issues can be discussed. The understanding of the past of IR – how it started, how it 'evolved' and how the present IR came to be – informs understandings of what 'debates' become possible and what 'debates' cannot be considered.

The 'great debates' are stories told and retold, myths that have been established and invented 'traditions' that have come to define the field. In its attempt to write its own history, IR has also constructed it. This approach draws the boundaries of IR discourse and establishes the hegemony of specific concepts and perspectives and determines the hierarchies within the discursive field. The writing of history constructs the past and in that process disciplines it. The 'traditional' or the dominant story of IR works to define not only the field but also the important concepts, the evolutions, the schools and the perspectives included and excluded. As such, the re-writing of disciplinary histories also works to redefine the boundaries of what is deemed as possible and impossible within debates about international relations. In that sense, the questions that can be asked are defined through the boundaries of the story of IR. The tracing of the manifestations of Eurocentrism and the strategies to question Eurocentrism enable new geographies and imaginations of boundaries to emerge. Thus, the re-writing is not a fixed one but rather is one that focuses on the questions being posed. The question being posed in this book is about Eurocentrism in International Relations. Writing about the problem of Eurocentrism necessitates the reimagining of disciplinary and theoretical borders, in order to trace its different manifestations and criticisms across disciplinary boundaries and geopolitical knowledges.

Historiographies of IR attempt to re-write the 'dominant' stories of the field but end up reproducing the dominance of the centre and the Eurocentric accounts of International Relations. In outlining the aims of his book, Ashworth summarizes his goals as follows: 'to understand the development, richness, complexities, silences, contradictions and form of this fundamentally Eurocentric (and, certainly since the 1890s, Anglocentric) project we call international thought as a thing in itself'.[15] As a consequence, he readily admits to his study being Eurocentric 'in the sense that it is studying a product of European (or western) civilisation'.[16] This argument is reminiscent of Bull and Watson's rationale for the Eurocentrism of their study of the international system:

> The present international political structure of the world – founded upon the division of mankind and of the earth into separate states, their acceptance of one another's sovereignty, of principles of law regulating their coexistence and

co-operation, and of diplomatic conventions facilitating their intercourse – is, at least in its most basic features, the legacy of Europe's now vanished ascendancy. Because it was in fact Europe and not America, Asia, or Africa that first dominated and, in so doing, unified the world, it is not our perspective but the historical record itself that can be called Eurocentric.[17]

This rationale rests on a circular logic whereby because the 'centre' of events, ideas and concepts is Europe, accounts that take Europe as centre are inevitably Eurocentric. As works concentrating on the connected nature of the development of international society have demonstrated, the 'East' is not absent from the story of the development of international society. As Seth states: 'Any satisfactory account of the emergence of the modern international system cannot simply chart how an international society that developed in the West radiated outwards, but rather seek to explore the ways in which international society was shaped by the interactions between Europe and those it colonized'.[18] Furthermore, it needs to be underlined that this Eurocentric account of the international system constitutes the field and defines the boundaries of the discourse on IR. The silences and omissions from the story of the development of the international system condition the manner in which concepts of the international, security, sovereignty and democracy are defined. As such, retelling the story reproduces the implicit hierarchies inscribed within the narrative and continues to silence alternative voices. It needs to be highlighted 'how some of the critical conceptual binding blocks of IR discourse – sovereignty, property, nationness, and international law, to mention some – were all emergent in the encounter between the West and the third world'.[19] There have thus been a myriad of works that underline how international society, sovereignty and international law emerged as a result of the encounter between the 'East' and the 'West', questioning the centrality of the West within accounts of international relations[20]; yet, this has had very little effect on stories of International Relations.[21]

The book intervenes in these debates by arguing that International Relations needs to be re-written by taking as its focal point the questions that it asks of itself and the connections they reveal. As such, the story of the Eurocentrism of International Relations needs to be told in and through disciplinary formations and geopolitical contexts. The starting premise of the book is to argue for the necessity to read and write by connecting, relating and perhaps ultimately breaking down different classificatory archives of knowledge.

CONNECTING INTERNATIONAL RELATIONS

'Oh, East is East and West is West, and never the twain shall meet' is the famous line from Rudyard Kipling's 'Ballad of the East and West'.[22] Is that really so, one might ask, especially considering that at the time these words were written 'the East and West were engaged in a seriously protracted encounter'.[23] Moreover, the existence of the idea that there is an East and a West is predicated on a 'meeting', an 'encounter' that has created these divisions and categories. The continued employment of East and West works to reproduce and reify the initial impulses behind such categorizations. The challenge that the writings of history, of international relations and of sociology face is the question of writing without continuing to reify and reproduce the categories of 'East' and 'West'.[24] Even as the 'West' is criticized for its imperial past, for its neocolonial present, for the Eurocentric categories through which the world has been made intelligible and for the silences it has created in our understandings of the past, present and future, it is always through the 'West' that the analysis proceeds. The 'East' comes in as the 'other', the 'mystical', the 'spiritual' and as the one outside of the projects of modernity and Enlightenment. The West remains the main actor and the East the victim. East remains the East and West remains the West, even as we attempt to question the West and bring in the East. Said refers to the way in which empire functions 'as a reference, as a point of definition', whereby it is 'only marginally visible' in fiction, 'much like the servants in grand households and in novels, whose work is taken for granted but scarcely ever more than named' and as such remains as 'people on whom the economy and polity sustained by empire depend, but whose reality has not historically or culturally required attention'.[25] 'The 'East' functions in a similar manner, as a reference point, in the background, visible only when the story of the West warrants it, and, as a consequence, the usage of the 'East' continues to be about the story of the 'West'. Eurocentrism is problematized for the Western actor, and the Western actor is given the role of fixing this issue at the 'centre' with the underlying assumption that if the 'problem' is fixed at the 'centre', then the problem is solved. As such, it needs to be underlined that 'translating modernity is not simply an act of assimilating meanings and practices, and neither is it solely an act of resistance' but rather 'domination, resistance, appropriation and transformation have to be understood as congenitally entangled in this moment of knowledge production'.[26]

The aim of the book is to present a possible way of reading and re-writing the Eurocentrism of International Relations. The method proposed for such an endeavour is to re-write histories of the manifestations and criticisms of Eurocentrism through 'connected histories'.[27] As Bhambra argues, 'Any model that posits a world historical centre from which developments diffuse outwards is problematic' and, as such, 'what is needed is a "connected histories" approach with a decentred conception of "totality"; decentred not just spatially, but also conceptually'.[28] Thus, the aim is to not 'only compare from within our boxes, but spend some time and effort to transcend them, not by comparison alone but by seeking out the at-times fragile threads that connected the globe'.[29] The connectivities and circulation of ideas, concepts and practices encapsulate not 'dissemination' or 'transmission' but rather the 'processes of encounter, power and resistance, negotiation, and reconfiguration'.[30] It should be noted that the connections and conversations are not absent from the 'past' but in our renderings of them. Susan Buck-Morss points this out with respect to the Haitian Revolution.[31] The Haitian Revolution was the first slave revolt in history, and its message of emancipation was known in its time.[32] It being forgotten is a consequence of 'the disciplinary discourses through which knowledge of the past has been inherited'.[33] An example from the field of IR is Robert Vitalis's work and his excavation of the racial origins of international relations and marginalization of the 'Howard school' of international relations.[34] He points out that the Howard school made important critiques towards racial science and the relationship between racism and imperialism. Furthermore, the Howard school of international relations established connections 'with the theoreticians of liberation and the future leaders of independent Africa and the island nations of the Caribbean'.[35] As such, it needs to be underlined that 'invisible things are not necessarily "not-there": a void may be empty but not be a vacuum' and some 'absences are so stressed, so ornate, so planned, they call attention to themselves; arrest us with intentionality and purpose, like neighbourhoods that are defined by the population held away from them'.[36] In that sense, it is important to problematize those absences to reveal the connections that were held away from coming to the fore as the borders around disciplinary knowledges formed.[37] The idea though is not adding these absences back into the story but underlining that the absences have been constitutive of disciplinary formations.[38] Furthermore, these disciplinary formations preclude the story of the manifestations of Eurocentrism and the strategies developed to counter it. The focus of the book then is not the 'absences' that can be located in the past but have been forgotten within disciplinary formations, though this itself is an important project that has been receiving attention. The focus rather is on how Eurocentrism manifests itself in and between disciplinary formations and how the critique of Eurocentrism moves in and between disciplinary formations. The aim is thus to place International Relations within a framework of interconnectedness.

ORGANIZATION OF THE BOOK

The book thus aims to contribute to the present ways of writing the Eurocentrism of International Relations. The focus will be on both the manifestations of Eurocentrism and the criticisms of Eurocentrism in and through disciplinary formations and geopolitical contexts.

Section I of the book will focus on manifestations of Eurocentrism. The main argument is that Eurocentrism of the 'field' of international relations and its narratives should not be discussed through taking the 'field' as an unproblematic unit, but rather through questioning its borders and how Eurocentrism travels in and out of the 'field'. The disciplinary formations discussed in this chapter are International Relations and History. The relationship between history and international relations is a continuing one, and as such how Eurocentrism manifests itself in and through these disciplines needs to be central to the discussion about bringing history into international relations. Chapter 1 focuses on the issues related to 'bringing in history' into the field of international relations problematizing the borders in and between disciplines. Chapter 2 focuses on the manifestations of Eurocentrism in the historiographical debates on the Cold War, both in the 'centre' and in the 'periphery'. Chapter 3 focuses on the 'past' and traces the manifestations of Eurocentrism within the archives. The Eurocentrism that manifests itself is primarily historical in the sense that 'world politics is taken to be happening almost exclusively in Europe, or latterly in the Northern hemisphere', and the entry of the Third World into debates 'is derivative of European developments and driven by great-power competition and the diffusion of European ideas and institutions'.[39] The example of Turkey is utilized because of the way in which 'Turkey' in general is written as inhabiting an 'in-between' space, as an actor bridging the East and the West, which through discussions of 'Turkey' continues to erect boundaries. 'Turkey', in that sense, is an interesting case of reflecting on a variety of anxieties[40] with respect to locating the 'non-West'. The section then aims at discussing the different ways in which Eurocentrism manifests itself in and between disciplinary formations and geopolitical contexts.

Section II of the book focuses on criticisms of Eurocentrism. The aim is to trace the connections in and between theoretical strategies developed to criticize Eurocentrism. The section underlines the discussions between different disciplines and geopolitical knowledges regarding the postcolonial condition and Eurocentrism. This section is divided into two parts. Chapter 4, 'Coloniality, Decoloniality, Postcoloniality', presents an intertwined and connected intellectual story of the theoretical perspectives that have questioned Eurocentrism and the process of knowledge production. This chapter thus works to underline the different manifestations of strategies to counter Eurocentrism in and through disciplines and geopolitical knowledges. Chapter 5, 'Constructing the Non-Western', focuses on the way these strategies travelled into the field of International Relations. This section aims to problematize the issue presented by Subrahmanyam, which is to 'redraw maps that emerge from the problematics we wish to study rather than insert problematics to fit our pre-existing categories'.[41] It will be underlined that the map of the strategies to counter Eurocentrism should be taken rather than taking these strategies and making them fit the field of International Relations.

The book concludes by arguing for a greater engagement with connections between disciplinary boundaries and geopolitical knowledges and underlines the importance of looking beyond linear and bounded histories. The aim of the book is to present a possible way of rereading and re-writing disciplinary histories, specifically focusing on the story of Eurocentrism and on how manifestations and criticisms of Eurocentrism need to be thought in and through disciplinary formations and geopolitical knowledges.

NOTES

1. Brian C. Schmidt, *The Political Discourse of Anarchy: A Disciplinary History of International Relations* (Albany: SUNY Press, 1998); Brian Schmidt, ed. *International Relations and the First Great Debate* (London and New York: Routledge, 2013). Joel Quirk and Darshan Vigneswaran, 'The Construction of an Edifice: The Story of a First Great Debate', *Review of International Studies* 31, no. 01 (2005): 89–97 ; Lucian M. Ashworth, 'Did the Realist-Idealist Great Debate Really Happen? A Revisionist History of International Relations', *International Relations* 16, no. 1 (2002): 33–51; 'Where Are the Idealists in Interwar International Relations?', *Review of International Studies* 32, no. 02 (2006): 291–308; Duncan Bell, 'Writing the World: Disciplinary History and Beyond', *International Affairs* 85, no. 1 (2009): 3–22; Nicolas Guilhot, 'The Realist Gambit: Postwar American Political Science and the Birth of IR Theory', *International Political Sociology* 2, no. 4 (2008): 281–304.

2. Arlene B. Tickner and David L. Blaney, eds. *Thinking International Relations Differently* (London and New York: Routledge, 2013); Amitav Acharya and Barry Buzan, eds. *Non-Western International Relations Theory: Perspectives on and Beyond Asia* (London: Routledge, 2010); John Hobson, *The Eurocentric Conception of World Politics: Western International Theory, 1760–2010* (Cambridge: Cambridge University Press, 2012); Robbie Shilliam, ed. *International Relations and Non-Western Thought* (London and New York: Routledge, 2011); L. H. M. Ling, *The Dao of World Politics: Towards a Post-Westphalian Worldist International Relations* (New York and London: Routledge, 2013).

3. Samir Amin, *Eurocentrism* (New York: NYU Press, 1989); Ella Shohat and Robert Stam, *Unthinking Eurocentrism: Multiculturalism and the Media* (London and New York: Routledge, 2014); Hobson, *The Eurocentric Conception of World Politics: Western International Theory, 1760–2010*; Siba N'Zatioula Grovogui, *Beyond Eurocentrism and Anarchy: Memories of International Order and Institutions* (London: Palgrave Macmillan, 2006); Pınar Bilgin, *The International in Security, Security in the International* (London: Routledge, 2016).

4. Immanuel Wallerstein, 'Eurocentrism and Its Avatars: The Dilemmas of Social Science', *Sociological Bulletin* 46, no. 1 (1997): 21–39.

5. Meera Sabaratnam, 'Avatars of Eurocentrism in the Critique of the Liberal Peace', *Security Dialogue* 44, no. 3 (2013): 259–278.

6. 'Avatars of Eurocentrism in the Critique of the Liberal Peace'.

7. Sanjay Subrahmanyam, *Explorations in Connected Histories: From the Tagus to the Ganges* (Oxford: Oxford University Press, 2005), 4.

8. In the text, International Relations (IR) refers to the discipline, whereas 'international relations' refers to the events of world politics.

9. John Hobson, *The Eastern Origins of Western Civilization* (Cambridge: Cambridge University Press, 2004), 10.

10. Tarak Barkawi and Mark Laffey, 'The Postcolonial Moment in Security Studies', *Review of International Studies* 32, no. 2 (2006): 329–352; Shogo Suzuki, *Civilization and Empire: China and Japan's Encounter with European International Society* (London: Routledge, 2009); John Hobson, 'Provincializing Westphalia: The Eastern Origins of Sovereignty', *International Politics* 46, no. 6 (2009): 671–690.

11. On performativity, see Mark Laffey, 'Locating Identity: Performativity, Foreign Policy and State Action', *Review of International Studies* 26, no. 3 (2000); James Loxley, *Performativity* (New York: Routledge, 2006): 429–444; Judith Butler, *Excitable Speech : A Politics of the Performative* (New York: Routledge, 1997); Cynthia Weber, 'Performative States', *Millennium-Journal of International Studies* 27, no. 1 (1998): 77–95.

12. Ole Waever, 'The Rise and Fall of the Inter-Paradigm Debate', in *International Theory: Positivism and Beyond*, ed. Ken Booth and Marysia Zalewski Steve Smith (Cambridge: Cambridge University Press, 1996), 175.

13. 'The Rise and Fall of the Inter-Paradigm Debate'.

14. 'The Rise and Fall of the Inter-Paradigm Debate', 175.

15. Lucian Ashworth, *A History of International Thought: From the Origins of the Modern State to Academic International Relations* (London: Routledge, 2014), 7.

16. *A History of International Thought: From the Origins of the Modern State to Academic International Relations*.

17. Hedley Bull and Adam Watson, 'Introduction', in *The Expansion of International Society*, ed. Hedley Bull and Adam Watson (Oxford: Clarendon Press, 1984), 2.

18. Sanjay Seth, 'Postcolonial Theory and the Critique of International Relations', *Millennium-Journal of International Studies* 40, no. 1 (2011), 174.

19. Sankaran Krishna, 'Race, Amnesia, and the Education of International Relations', *Alternatives* 26, no. 4 (2001), 408.

20. Antony Anghie, *Imperialism, Sovereignty and the Making of International Law*, vol. 37 (Cambridge: Cambridge University Press, 2007); Sundhya Pahuja, *Decolonising International Law: Development, Economic Growth and the Politics of Universality*, vol. 86 (Cambridge: Cambridge University Press, 2011); Siba N'Zatioula Grovogui, *Sovereigns, Quasi Sovereigns, and Africans: Race and Self-Determination in International Law*, Borderlines (Minneapolis, MN: University of Minnesota Press, 1996); Suzuki, *Civilization and Empire: China and Japan's Encounter with European International Society*; Ayse Zarakol, *After Defeat: How the East Learned to Live with the West* (Cambridge: Cambridge University Press, 2010); Edward Keene, *Beyond the Anarchical Society: Grotius, Colonialism and Order in World Politics* (Cambridge: Cambridge University Press, 2002); Robbie Shilliam, 'What About Marcus Garvey? Race and the Transformation of Sovereignty Debate', *Review of International Studies* 32, no. 3 (2006): 379–400.

21. For notable exceptions, see Robert Vitalis, 'The Noble American Science of Imperial Relations and Its Laws of Race Development', *Comparative Studies in Society and History* 52, no. 4 (2010): 903–938; *White World Order, Black Power Politics: The Birth of American International Relations* (Ithaca, New York: Cornell University Press, 2015); David Long and Brian C. Schmidt, *Imperialism and Internationalism in the Discipline of International Relations* (Cambridge: Cambridge University Press, 2005).

22. Rudyard Kipling, *The Collected Poems of Rudyard Kipling* (Ware: Wordsworth Editions, 1994), 245.

23. Uma Narayan, 'Essence of Culture and a Sense of History: A Feminist Critique of Cultural Essentialism', *Hypatia* 13, no. 2 (1998), 89.

24. Stuart Hall, 'The West and the Rest: Discourse and Power', in *Formations of Modernity*, ed. Stuart Hall and Bram Gieben (Cambridge: Cambridge Polity Press, 1992).

25. Edward W. Said, *Culture and Imperialism* (New York: Vintage Books, 1994), 63.

26. Robbie Shilliam, ed. *International Relations and Non-Western Thought: Imperialism, Colonialism and Investigations of Global Modernity* (London: Routledge, 2010), 20.

27. For the way in which 'connected histories' has been brought into sociology, see Gurminder Bhambra, *Rethinking Modernity : Postcolonialism and the Sociological Imagination* (Basingstoke: Palgrave, 2007); Gurminder K Bhambra, 'Historical Sociology, International Relations and Connected Histories', *Cambridge Review of International Affairs* 23, no. 1 (2010): 127–143; *Connected Sociologies* (Bloomsbury Publishing, 2014).

28. 'Historical Sociology, International Relations and Connected Histories', 128–129.

29. Sanjay Subrahmanyam, 'Connected Histories: Notes Towards a Reconfiguration of Early Modern Eurasia', *Modern Asian Studies* 31, no. 3 (1997), 761–762.

30. Kapil Raj, 'Beyond Postcolonialism ... and Postpositivism: Circulation and the Global History of Science', *Isis* 104, no. 2 (2013), 343.

31. Susan Buck-Morss, *Hegel, Haiti, and Universal History* (Pittsburgh: University of Pittsburgh Press, 2009).

32. Ada Ferrer, *Freedom's Mirror* (Cambridge: Cambridge University Press, 2014); Laurent Dubois, *Avengers of the New World* (Cambridge, MA: Harvard University Press, 2005); Julia Gaffield, *Haitian Connections in the Atlantic World: Recognition after Revolution* (Chapel Hill, NC: UNC Press Books, 2015); Matthew J. Clavin, *Toussaint Louverture and the American Civil War: The Promise and Peril of a Second Haitian Revolution* (Philadelphia: University of Pennsylvania Press, 2010).

33. Buck-Morss, *Hegel, Haiti, and Universal History*, 50.

34. Robert Vitalis, *White World Order, Black Power Politics: The Birth of American International Relations* (Ithaca, New York: Cornell University Press, 2015)

35. *White World Order, Black Power Politics: The Birth of American International Relations*.

36. Toni Morrison, 'Unspeakable Things Unspoken: The Afro-American Presence in American Literature', *Michigan Quarterly Review* 28, no. Winter (1989): 1–34.

37. Siba N'Zatioula Grovogui, 'Mind, Body, and Gut! Elements of a Postcolonial Human Rights Discourse', in *Decolonising International Relations*, ed. Branwyn Gruffyd Jones (Maryland: Rowman & Littlefield, 2006): 179–196; Robbie Shilliam, 'What the Haitian Revolution Might Tell Us About Development, Security, and the Politics of Race', *Comparative Studies in Society and History* 50, no. 3 (2008): 778–808; Robbie Shilliam, '"Open the Gates Mek We Repatriate": Caribbean Slavery, Constructivism, and Hermeneutic Tensions', *International Theory* 6, no. 02 (2014): 349–372; 'Intervention and Colonial-Modernity: Decolonising the Italy/Ethiopia Conflict through Psalms 68: 31', *Review of International Studies* 39, no. 5 (2013): 1131–1147; Gurminder K. Bhambra, 'A Sociological Dilemma: Race, Segregation and Us Sociology', *Current Sociology* 62, no. 4 (2014): 472–492; Aldon Morris, *The Scholar Denied: Web Du Bois and the Birth of Modern Sociology* (Berkeley: University of California Press, 2015).

38. Pınar Bilgin, 'The "Western-Centrism" of Security Studies: "Blind Spot" or Constitutive Practice?', *Security Dialogue* 41, no. 6 (2010): 615–622.

39. Barkawi and Laffey, 'The Postcolonial Moment in Security Studies', 334–335.

40. Pınar Bilgin and Başak Ince, 'Security and Citizenship in the Global South: In/Securing Citizens in Early Republican Turkey (1923–1946)', *International Relations* 29, no. 4 (2015): 500–520; Pınar Bilgin and Ali Bilgiç, 'Turkey and Eu/Rope: Discourses of Inspiration/Anxiety in Turkey's Foreign Policy', *Review of European Studies* 4, no. 3 (2012): 111–124.

41. Subrahmanyam, *Explorations in Connected Histories: From the Tagus to the Ganges*.

Section I

MANIFESTATIONS OF EUROCENTRISM

The aim of the book is to problematize the ways in which the story of Eurocentrism is written in the field of International Relations. The present section entitled 'Manifestations of Eurocentrism' will focus on manifestations of Eurocentrism in and between disciplines and geopolitical knowledges.

Chapter 1, entitled 'History' in International Relations, will focus on the relationship between the disciplines of history and International Relations. The chapter will underline that the past *as it happened* cannot be recovered and reconstructed. In that sense, a story of the past is transformed into history. Furthermore, the chapter will discuss the relationship between history and historiography and how the writing of history constructs the borders of possible debates about the 'past'.

Chapter 2, entitled 'International Relations in History', will focus on how Eurocentrism manifests itself in historiographical debates on the Cold War and how the boundaries of these historiographical debates are reproduced in the context of Turkey. The chapter aims to underline how the manner in which historiographical debates 'write' and 'make' the Cold War also determines the borders of the 'history' that comes to be accepted as the past.

Chapter 3, entitled 'The Past as Experienced', will focus on the manifestations of Eurocentrism that can be 'read' through the traces of the 'past'. The chapter aims to underline how different hierarchies were reproduced between the West and Turkey in discussions about the international system, the importance and centrality of the United States, the threat of communism and the Soviet Union.

The section aims to underline through the example of History and International Relations the different manifestations of Eurocentrism in and through disciplinary formations and geopolitical contexts. The section will argue that the story of Eurocentrism has to take into account the ways in which Eurocentrism manifests not just in one disciplinary formation or geopolitical context but in and through disciplinary formations and geopolitical contexts as well, underscoring the need to approach it through connected histories.

Chapter 1

'History' in International Relations

The aim of this chapter is to enter into conversation with the problem of the discipline of history and to understand the relationship between 'the past', 'history' and 'historiography'. In that vein, the first part of the chapter will discuss what history is and how it is different from the 'past'. The second part of the chapter will focus on how the 'past' is transformed into history. The third part of the chapter will elaborate on how to understand historiography and historiographical debates.

The field of International Relations (IR) in the last few decades has undergone what has been dubbed as the 'historical turn' or the 'historiographical turn'.[1] The aim has been to bring 'history' back in to IR as a way of overcoming the shortcomings of the field, since the misuse of history was identified as one of the persistent problems of the field. Barry Buzan and Richard Little identify five shortcomings:

> presentism, or the tendency to view the past in terms of the present; ahistoricism, or the insistence that there are trans-historical concepts that allow us to identify universal regularities; Eurocentrism, or the privileging of European experience in our understanding of international relations; anarchophilia, or the propensity to equate international relations with the existence of an anarchic system; and state-centrism, or the preoccupation with the state at the expense of other international actors.[2]

Three of the five shortcomings, presentism, ahistoricism and Eurocentrism, are directly linked to the role history plays in the field. John Hobson in similar vein identifies two main shortcomings: 'tempocentrism' and 'chronofetishism'. Tempocentric ahistoricism extrapolates the characteristics of the present system and actors 'back in time', which 'smooths out historical

15

ruptures and social differences'.[3] Problematizing this enables a rethinking of
the 'specific and unique origins of the *modern* international system'.[4] Chronofetishism focuses on the present by 'bracketing or ignoring the past' and
portraying 'the present as a natural, spontaneous, self-constituting entity that
is … eternalized'.[5] Both discussions underline the misuse of history as something that needs to be remedied in the field. As a consequence, there have
been increasing number of works that historicize concepts, events, issues and
the field in general. History is being used as an explanatory tool to deepen the
understanding within the field, yet history as a concept that also needs to be
explained and engaged critically is being overlooked.[6] Even though history
has been brought in, it is often overlooked which history is being brought in,
thus privileging one understanding of history over others, as a result of which
'the discourse of the historical turn actually runs the risk of facilitating continued hegemony of an ahistorical or at worst anti-historical research culture
in IR'.[7] History should not be just brought in as an unproblematic concept
but rather engaged with critically. As Vaughan-Williams states: 'In order
to historicize the concepts, logics and theories with which we study international relations it is necessary not to bring "history" but more specifically the
"problem of history" into the discipline'.[8]

The concept of 'history' is not unproblematic and has always been contested and widely discussed. Overlooking these debates privileges one version of the definition of history rather than opening up for discussion of its
contested nature. The discussions revolving around the 'problem of history'
can be divided into three perspectives: reconstructionism, constructionism
and deconstructionism.[9] Reconstructionism argues that primary sources can
lead to achieving the Rankean aim of knowing the past 'as it actually happened'. Marwick, one of the leading proponents of reconstructionism, defines
history as 'a body of knowledge about the human past based on the systemic
study of sources'.[10] Constructionism consists of a wide array of 'schools' 'that
appeal to general laws in historical explanation'.[11] French Annalistes, modernization theory and the Marxist or neo-Marxist approaches are all included
under the heading of constructionism. According to constructionism, 'History
can explain the past only when the evidence is placed within a preexisting
explanatory framework that allows for the calculation of general rules of
human action'.[12] Deconstructionist history questions the assumption of writing history 'as it actually was' and focuses on a postmodern understanding
of history.[13] The main proponents of this perspective are Hayden White,[14]
Dominick LaCapra,[15] Keith Jenkins[16] and F. R. Ankersmit,[17] among many
others. Deconstructionism views 'history and the past as a complex series
of literary products that derive their chains of meaning(s) or significations
from the nature of narrative structure (or forms of representation) as much
as from other culturally provided ideological factors'.[18] This brief sketch[19]

demonstrates clearly how erroneous it is to automatically bring in history as if it was a neutral concept.

Bringing in history into the discussion also needs to mean bringing the following questions into the discussion:

> Who gets to tell the story of the past? What are the implications of where the story starts and stops; which characters and topics are included and excluded; what 'voice' is adopted; what metaphors provide structure? … What dynamic relationship does each of us bring to the process of meaning and representation? Conscious or unconscious decisions about form, voice, and metaphor shape the content of historical stories, and many interpretive differences in historiography (especially in the international field) arise from this 'content of the form' and from inescapable issues of subjectivity and partiality.[20]

The aim of this chapter is to discuss the problem of history and attempt to find an answer to the question, 'What is history?' The first section will engage critically with the concept of history and attempt to elaborate on questions such as, What is history? Can the past be known? Can history ever recover the past? The second section will discuss the role of the narrative and how the past is transformed into history. The third section will focus on what historiography means and how concepts, periods and historiographical debates should be approached.

WHAT IS HISTORY?[21]

Is history the writing of the past 'as it happened'? The primary question 'What is history?' needs to be opened up in order to capture the complicated nature of its meaning into 'What is the past?' Is the past and history the same or are they different? Does the 'it' in the Rankean dictum of 'as it really happened' actually exist?

In its simplest terms, the past is what has happened and *history is a retelling of a story of what has happened*. There are a series of qualifications here:

1. History is not *the telling* of a story but *the retelling*. The past cannot be recreated in its entirety within a story and as such is always incomplete; history can retell a part of the past but never recreate it.
2. History is not the retelling *of the story* of the past but a retelling *of a story of* the past. Since history cannot capture the past in its entirety, it is always a partial story of what has happened and is never a final, closed, settled account of the past.

   All the actors involved do not experience events in the same manner. The past does not have clearly delineated beginnings, middles and ends;

it does not occur in a linear manner. It does not exist as a story to be told; the past has to be fashioned into a story. The events and actors of the past are transformed into an easily followable story, and it is that story that is history rather than the past itself. This point leads to two further elaborations on what history is:

3. If history is the *retelling of a story* and the past as it was cannot be captured, then every retelling is a construct.

4. If every retelling is a construct, then this construction is not based on recreating the past but according to the questions asked in the present. The retelling of a story necessitates that the past be fashioned into a story with a beginning, middle and end, with answers to questions such as, why is this important? The past is not lived in narrative form; it is written as such. This writing is as much about the facts of the past as about the concerns of the present. The questions the historians direct towards the text are the questions conditioned by the present.

5. Because the past is not retrieved, the writing of history is oriented in the present and related to the questions we have about the past in the present. As such, 'Is it possible that the past unfolded as a particular kind of narrative the first time around and can we recover it more or less intact, or are we only selecting and imposing an emplotment or story line on it derived from our own present? Are stories lived in the past or just told in the present?'[22] Whatever is lived in the past is not the story told in the present; history is the story of the past told in the present and for the present.

In that sense, the question 'what is history?' needs to be opened up even further. As discussed, in order to understand what history is, it is necessary to elaborate on its differences with the 'past' and on the relationship between the past and history and to ask the question, what is the past? If the past is not retrievable and history is a retelling of a past, the next question becomes, why retell the past? It is not only 'what is history?' but also 'what is the purpose of history?' or rather 'who is history for?' Similar to Cox's oft-cited quote, 'Theory is always for someone',[23] Jenkins states, 'History is never for itself, it is always for someone'.[24]

6. History is not only and maybe not even primarily about events, issues, debates and actors of the past but about what their story means for the issues, debates, events and actors in the present. As Jenkins states:

> The fact that history *per se* is an ideological construct means that it is constantly being re-worked and re-ordered by all those who are variously affected by power relationships; because the dominated as well as the dominant also have their versions of the past to legitimate their practices, versions which have to be excluded as improper from any place on the agenda of the dominant discourse. In that sense re-orderings of the messages to be delivered (often many such re-orderings are referred to academically as

'controversies') just have to be constructed continuously because the needs of the dominant/subordinate are constantly being re-worked in the real world as they seek to mobilise people(s) in support of their interests. History is forged in such conflict and clearly these conflicting needs for history impinge upon the debates (struggle for ownership) as to what history is.[25]

7. History is not only a construct but also an ideological construct. If it is always written with a purpose and for someone, then the fashioning of the story is determined by the questions and frames necessitated by the purpose of the story.
8. History is a series of discourses that work to define, categorize, periodize, limit, silence and make the past intelligible. As history is written for some purpose, then the transformation of the past into history and the definitions, categories, periodizations and inclusions or exclusions of that written work are there to reinforce, reproduce and reify the discursive spaces of a specific rendering of the past.
9. The past is not what is in contestation but the historiographical renderings of it. History is a retelling of a story of the past with a purpose in mind that works within already existing discourses about the past. Thus, historical debates are not debates about the past itself but rather a debate between the discourses of the past. In that sense, 'History results not from the debate about the past reality as such, but from competing narrative proposals about the nature and possible meanings of past events,'[26] and when 'a narrative proposal has achieved a more or less universal acceptance (like "the Cold War" or "the Industrial Revolution") it becomes concretized as past reality. *It is no longer a narrative proposal, but has become the past*'.[27]

As discussed so far, history is not the past and its acceptance as being representative of the past is the result of the dominance and acceptance of the discourses of the past.[28] This section attempted to open up the definition of history primarily by underlying the difference between the past and history. Furthermore, only asking, 'What is history?' is not sufficient in questioning the nature of history; what also needs to be asked is, 'Who is history for?' The writing of history is always informed by some purpose that conditions the questions the historian asks of the past, the text and the archive and that transforms the past into history. The next section will elaborate further on how the past is transformed into history.

TRANSFORMATION OF THE PAST

The previous section focused upon answering the question, 'What is history?' and discussed the way in which the past and history are not the same.

This section will elaborate on how the past transforms into history. History is written through the narrativization of past events. Narrative 'is a discourse that places disparate events in an understandable order',[29] and this order does not exist in the evidence but is imposed upon the events by the historian.

Hayden White, in *The Content of the Form*, reproduces the following list from the *Annals of Saint Gall*, which chronicles events that occurred in Gaul:

709.   Hard winter. Duke Gottfried died.
710.   Hard year and deficient in crops.
711.
712.   Flood everywhere.
713.
714.   Pippin, mayor of the palace, died.
715.   716. 717
718.   Charles devastated the Saxon with great destruction
719.
720.   Charles fought against the Saxons
721.   Theudo drove the Saracens out of Aquitaine
722.   Great crops
723.
724.
725.   Saracens came for the first time.
726.
727.
728.
729.
730.
731.   Blessed Bede, the presbyter, died.
732.   Charles fought against the Saracens at Poitiers on Saturday.
733.
734.

The list is of the 'past'; these events did happen when the annalist entered them, yet the list is not a historical account mainly because it does not have a story or a plot. The past events have not been narrativized. First, there is no hierarchy among events. The great crops of 722 has an entry similar to the entry on Charles fighting against the Saracens. Secondly, there is no causality between the events. There is no attempt to understand the implications of Duke Gottfried's death in 709. Thus, White states:

> Modern commentators have remarked on the fact that the annalist recorded the Battle of Poiters of 732 but failed to note the battle of Tours which occurred in the same year and which as every schoolboy knows was one of 'the ten greatest battles of the world history'. But even if the annalist had known of Tours, what principle or rule of meaning would have required him to record it? It is only

from our knowledge of the subsequent history of Western Europe that we can presume to rank events in terms of their world-historical significance.[31]

The above list chronicles a set of events during a given time and place and imparts knowledge about the past. What this list does not do is tell the story of the past; hence, it is not history as such. The events in the chronicle are assigned importance or placed within a causal relationship when the events are narrativized by the historian. Past events do not come with hierarchy of significance or causal relationships inscribed into them; the historian imposes it on them. An example from the Cold War[32] about the hierarchization of events might put this point in context. A list of events between 1945 and 1950 might look as follows:

- 'February 1945 – Yalta Conference[33]
- April 1945 – Death of President Franklin Roosevelt
- May 1945 – End of the Second World War in Europe
- September 1945 – Ho Chi Minh proclaims Vietnam an independent republic
- February 1946 – George F. Kennan writes the Long Telegram[34]
- March 1946 – Churchill's 'Iron Curtain' speech[35]
- April 1946 – North Atlantic Treaty establishing the North Atlantic Treaty Organization is signed
- July 1946 – Philippines gains independence from the United States
- March 1947 – The US President Harry Truman gives speech announcing the 'Truman Doctrine'[36]
- June 1947 – Secretary of State George Marshall's announcement of an economic aid plan
- July 1947 – Congress passes the National Security Act[37]
- February 1948 – Communist takeover in Czechoslovakia
- June 1948 – Berlin Blockade[38]
- August 1949 – Soviet Union detonates first atomic bomb
- October 1949 – Communist Mao Zedong takes control of China and establishes the People's Republic of China
- June 1950 – Korean War'

In order to make these series of events into a story, it is necessary to have a central subject, a geographical centre and a proper beginning in time. The central subject of these events can be the Cold War or the US foreign policy or US–Soviet rivalry. The geographical centre can shift based on which events are included or excluded from the story; the story can concentrate primarily on the events in Europe or in South-east Asia or in the Middle East. These events should have a proper beginning in time; the story might begin in 1917 with the Russian Revolution or in May 1945 with the end of the Second World War in Europe or in February 1946 with the writing of the George

Kennan's Long Telegram. As can be seen, a historian has a series of choices before him or her when approaching past events and facts.

There is a dual process of exclusion and inclusion of facts whereby the historian imposes his or her own narrative upon the facts. Some facts get excluded because there are always more facts than can be included in a narrative. Thus, all the events between 1945 and 1946 cannot be included in the story. The historian decides which events to include based on a series of considerations (the central subject, the geographical centre, etc.) and a series of questions (What happened next? How did it happen? Why did events occur in one way or another?). The second process of inclusion occurs because in order to 'reconstruct "what happened" in any given period of history, the historian inevitably must include in his narrative an account of some event or complex of events for which the facts that would permit a plausible explanation of its occurrence are lacking', meaning 'that the historian must "interpret" his materials by filling in the gaps in his information on inferential or speculative grounds'.[39]

To take the example of the facts of the period between 1945 and 1950 again, even though the events might remain the same, there are a series of possible narratives about the period in question depending upon how the hierarchy of significance is allocated:

Narrative 1: End of the Second World War, Marshall Plan, Truman Doctrine, Korean War
Narrative 2: End of the Second World War, Marshall Plan, Truman Doctrine, *Korean War*
Narrative 3: *End of the Second World War*, Marshall Plan, Truman Doctrine, Korean War
Narrative 4: End of the Second World War, *Marshall Plan*, Truman Doctrine, Korean War

The italics denote the narrative prioritizing one event in the narrative over others as the 'turning point'. This alters the rhythm of the story being told. If the narrative characterizes the death of Franklin Roosevelt as a turning point, then the story is that of President Truman's culpability at the start of the tensions with the Soviet Union, with the underlying assumption that had Roosevelt been alive this turn of events could have been avoided. If the Marshall Plan is taken as the starting point of tensions between the United States and the Soviet Union, then not only is the United States designated as being responsible for the rise of tensions between the two nations but, because it is the Marshall Plan that is singled out, capitalism and the opening up of markets also become an important factor in the story of the evolution of the Cold War. Taking the same period, including and excluding certain events, the number of possible narratives increases even more:

Narrative 5: End of the Second World War, Long Telegram, North Atlantic Treaty, National Security Act

Narrative 6: Yalta Conference, Ho Chi Minh proclaiming Vietnam as independent republic, Philippines's independence from the United States, Korean War

Narrative 7: End of the Second World War, communist takeover in Czechoslovakia, Berlin Blockade, Soviet Union's detonation of the first atomic bomb

The narratives include and exclude different events resulting in different stories about the past. The events have all happened, and evidence can be found in archives about all these events, yet their inclusion and exclusion and the construction of the narratives determine the story being told. Narrative 5 inscribes significance upon events belonging to the US foreign policy, including the NATO Treaty, and the National Security Act within the story makes the United States the main agent of the story and the establishment of the national security state an important factor in the development of the Cold War. Narrative 6 focuses on the 'Third World' and includes events that were absent from Narrative 5 whereby the developments in the international system are not solely explained from the perspective of the United States. Narrative 7, in direct opposition to Narrative 5, establishes the Soviet Union as the main agent of the developments in the international system, casting the expansion of communism as the main factor in the Cold War.

In order to transform the past into history, it is necessary to have an ordering of events and a plot. As discussed in this section, any series of events can be plotted differently depending on the choices the historian makes. These choices are related to the questions the historian asks of the past and also the explanatory strategies the historian employs in constructing their historical narrative. As Munslow states: 'History does not pre-exist in any body of facts that will allow unmediated access to *the* real past. History as opposed to the past, is a literary creation because it is always interpreted through textualized relics which themselves are only to be understood through layers of interpretation as the historian's facts'.[40] If history is a literary creation, a construct, a discourse on the past, then the meaning of historiography, historiographical debates, periods and concepts also need to be problematized. The next section will elaborate on what historiography means and how historiographical debates should be understood and analysed.

HISTORY AS HISTORIOGRAPHY

Problematizing the concept of history opens up the discussion for what historiography means as well. Thus, this section will focus on the meaning of historiography and the nature and role of historiographical debates, periods and concepts. As argued in earlier sections, history and the past are not equal. Past events are transformed into histories through a myriad of strategies such as explanation by emplotment, explanation by formal argument and explanation by ideology.[41] History is a discourse about the past, but it is not a static one; it is rather 'a shifting discourse constructed by the historians and that from the existence of the past no one reading is entailed: change the gaze, shift the perspective and new readings appear'.[42] All the possible readings of the past constitute historiography. In that sense, history is historiography because 'historiography is, in its essence, the making of narratives'.[43] Thus, 'history should be seen as what it manifestly is: a written discourse about the past and pre-existing narratives. Strictly speaking, then, there is no history only historiography defined as what we write about the past in order to understand it'.[44] It is because history is historiography that historiographical debates are not about facts of the past but about the interpretations of the past (history).

The differentiation between history and historiography is made to delimit the writing of history from *history-as-past* concept in that historiography is the history of historical writing and history is the writing of the past. This difference is constituted in order to constitute the past and History as a unified concept. The writing of history and historiography are coterminous in that the writing of history aims to 'fill in the blanks' of the history already written. The historiography of a subject provides the historian with the road map of what has been argued, the interpretations of events and possible future research areas. Historiography works to discipline the writing of history in that what is to be written, the 'periods' to be focused upon, the terminology of the interpretations are already determined and the historian only works to fill in the blanks and and/or reinterpret the past. Historiography constructs the borders of the historiographical debate and centres the understanding of the past on specific concepts, events and actors by privileging them and their interpretations. Furthermore, these debates construct periods and concepts of the past whereby the discourses of the past come to be seen as if they were the past silencing other possible renditions. Thus,

> if a narrative substance becomes widely accepted by the historians it sometimes looks *as if* there really was a Renaissance out there and it has been *discovered* But all that is actually going on here is the widespread acceptance of a *proposed* way of thinking through an ultimately arbitrary analytical category; nothing else.[45]

'Concepts' such as the Enlightenment, Renaissance or the Cold War are not concepts but 'images' or 'pictures' of the past because 'such concepts do *not* refer to things in or aspects of the past' but rather 'to narrative *interpretations* of the past'.[46] Thus, 'the "Renaissance", "the Cold War" and so on, are constructed or postulated, but have not been discovered in the historical past'.[47]

Historiography presents different views and interpretations about same or similar past events but in doing so distinguishes between history and History. Thus, 'although there are multiple interpretations, there is only one (hi)story; although there are partial histories, there is only one Great Story as their large context because there is only one Great past'.[48] This can be observed with respect to the Haitian Revolution and the French Revolution; there may be different renderings of events, but the Great Story is one that encompasses 'French Revolution', and within that story the Haitian Revolution does not have a place. The Haitian Revolution 'entered history with the peculiar characteristic of being unthinkable as it happened', and it could be read 'only with their ready-made categories, and these categories were incompatible with the idea of a slave revolution'.[49] In order to illustrate the way 'Great Story' works, Berkhofer gives the example of the blind sages describing the different parts of the elephant but all of them still describing the elephant.[50] The way in which history disciplines the past and constructs the basic tenets of historiography delimits the borders of what History is, whereby historiographical debates are conditioned by the assumption that the different interpretations of the elephant are all that can be analysed, limiting and excluding the possibilities of a myriad of Great Stories, such as the Haitian Revolution.

To conclude, problematizing history demonstrates how the 'differences' between history and historiography are constructed in a further attempt to discipline and centre the understanding of the past. History is used to order, define and limit the past, and, in turn, historiography is used to discipline history. Opening up the definition of history underlines the fact that both history and historiography are constructs, and as such both constructions are done for a purpose. Problematizing the meaning of history and as a consequence of historiography makes it possible to question the centring effect of history on the past.

CONCLUSION

This chapter has focused upon the different ways of understanding the past, history and historiography. The problem of history does not have a straightforward answer, nor is the writing of history solely about collecting facts.

History disciplines the past and the dominant discourses on the past that constitute the historiography of a period, a concept, an event discipline and delimit the boundaries of the field. As Munslow states:

> History is no longer defined then by the established categories of analysis – economic structures, competing nationalisms, political and cultural revolutions, the march and opposition of ideas, great men and women, periods of excess and ages of equipoise, republics and monarchies, empires and dynasties, famines and plagues – but instead by how societies interpret, imagine, create, control,

regulate and dispose of knowledge, especially through the claims of disciplines to truth, authority and certainty.[51]

History is a discourse used to discipline the past. It organizes, limits and defines the past according to the questions of the present. As such, entering into conversation with history means to think in and through the borders of both International Relations and History, underscoring the need to take them both as disciplines that need to be problematized. As such, writing the story of Eurocentrism within International Relations necessitates entering into conversation with History rather than bringing in history. The next two chapters of this section will thus demonstrate the manifestations of Eurocentrism in historiographical debates and the 'past' as experienced, underscoring the need to think in and through disciplinary formations in tracing problematiques.

NOTES

1. Stephen Hobden, 'Historical Sociology: Back to the Future of International Relations', in *Historical Sociology of International Relations*, ed. Stephen Hobden and John Hobson (Cambridge: Cambridge University Press, 2002); Duncan S. A. Bell, 'International Relations: The Dawn of a Historiographical Turn?', *The British Journal of Politics & International Relations* 3, no. 1 (2001): 115–126; George Lawson, 'The Eternal Divide? History and International Relations', *European Journal of International Relations* 18 (2010): 203–226.

2. Barry Buzan and Richard Little, 'World History and the Development of Non-Western International Relations Theory', in *Non-Western International Relations Theory: Perspectives on and Beyond Asia*, ed. Amitav Acharya and Barry Buzan (London: Routledge, 2010), 197.

3. 'World History and the Development of Non-Western International Relations Theory'.

4. 'World History and the Development of Non-Western International Relations Theory'.

5. 'World History and the Development of Non-Western International Relations Theory'.

6. For works that engage critically with the concept of history: Rob B. J. Walker, 'History and Structure in the Theory of International Relations', *Millennium-Journal of International Studies* 18, no. 2 (1989): 163–183; David Campbell, 'Metabosnia: Narratives of the Bosnian War', *Review of International Studies* 24, no. 02 (1998): 261–281; Patrick Finney, 'Still "Marking Time"? Text, Discourse and Truth in International History', *Review of International Studies* 27, no. 3 (2001): 291–308.

7 Nick Vaughan-Williams, 'International Relations and The problem of History', *Millennium-Journal of International Studies* 34, no. 1 (2005), 133.

8. 'International Relations and The problem of History'.

9. Alun Munslow, *Deconstructing History* (London; New York: Routledge, 1997).

10. Arthur Marwick (1998), "A Fetishism of Documents? The Salience of Source-Based History" cited in Alun Munslow, *The New History* (London: Routledge, 2003), 54.

11. Alun Munslow, *The New History* (London: Routledge, 2003), 54.

12. *The New History*, 24.

13. Hayden White, Dominik LaCapra, David Harlan, Allan Megill and Keith Jenkins are generally classified under 'deconstructionist history'.

14. Hayden White, *Metahistory: The Historical Imagination in Nineteenth-Century Europe* (Baltimore and London: Johns Hopkins University, 1973); *The Content of the Form: Narrative Discourse and Historical Representation* (Baltimore: John Hopkins University Press, 2009); *Tropics of Discourse: Essays in Cultural Criticism* (Baltimore: John Hopkins University Press, 1978).

15. Dominick LaCapra, *Writing History, Writing Trauma* (Baltimore: Johns Hopkins University Press, 2001).

16. Keith Jenkins, *On 'What Is History?'* (London: Routledge, 1995); *Rethinking History* (London: Routledge, 2003); *Refiguring History: New Thoughts on an Old Discipline* (London: Routledge, 2003).

17. F. R. Ankersmit, *Narrative Logic: A Semantic Analysis of the Historian's Language* (The Hague: M. Nijhoff, 1983); *Political Representation* (Stanford: Stanford University Press, 2002); *Historical Representation* (Stanford: Stanford University Press, 2002).

18. Munslow, *Deconstructing History*, 21.

19. It needs to be underlined that the outline provided here and the division of 'schools' and 'approaches' can be contested, and they were used in order to provide a bird's-eye view of the discussions about the nature of history. For further reading, see Michael Bentley, *Companion to Historiography* (London: Routledge, 1997); Georg G. Iggers, *Historiography in the Twentieth Century: From Scientific Objectivity to the Postmodern Challenge* (London: Wesleyan University Press, 1997); Keith Jenkins, *Postmodern History Reader* (London: Routledge, 1997).

20. Emily Rosenberg, 'Considering Borders', in *Explaining the History of American Foreign Relations*, ed. M. J. Hogan and T. G. Paterson (Cambridge: Cambridge University Press, 2004), 192.

21. Edward H. Carr, *What Is History* (New York: Vintage, 1967).

22. Munslow, *Deconstructing History*, 5.

23. Robert W. Cox, 'Social Forces, States and World Orders: Beyond International Relations Theory', *Millennium* 10, no. 2 (1981): 126–155.

24. Jenkins, *Rethinking History*, 21.

25. *Rethinking History*.

26. Munslow, *Deconstructing History*, 73.

27. *Deconstructing History*, 73.

28. More discussion on historiography and role of debates will be discussed in the third section of this chapter.

29. Munslow, *Deconstructing History*, 12.

30. White, *The Content of the Form: Narrative Discourse and Historical Representation*, 9.

31. *The Content of the Form: Narrative Discourse and Historical Representation*.

32. The periodization itself and the events chosen to exemplify the narrativization process are the ones that are accorded significance in the narratives of the 'Cold War', and the events are described in the same manner used in the narratives of the Cold War.

33. Yalta Conference, held from 4 to 11 February, was a meeting between the heads of the governments of the United States, United Kingdom and Soviet Union to discuss the reorganization of Europe in the aftermath of the Cold War.

34. George Kennan was the charge d'affaires of the United States in Moscow. He sent an 8,000-word telegram to the Department of State outlining his views on the Soviet Union and what the US policy should be.

35. Speech where Winston Churchill, the British prime minister, condemns the actions of the Soviet Union.

36. It was a doctrine announcing the intention to counter Soviet hegemony.

37. It was an act that restructured the military and intelligence agencies of the US government.

38. The Soviet Union blockade of the Allies' access to the sectors of Berlin when Germany was under occupation.

39 White, *Tropics of Discourse: Essays in Cultural Criticism*, 51.

40 Munslow, *Deconstructing History*, 33.

41. White, *Metahistory: The Historical Imagination in Nineteenth-Century Europe*.

42. Jenkins, *Rethinking History*, 16.

43. Munslow, *The New History*, 157.

44. *The New History.*

45. Jenkins, *Refiguring History: New Thoughts on an Old Discipline*, 50.

46. *Refiguring History: New Thoughts on an Old Discipline*, 93.

47. *Refiguring History: New Thoughts on an Old Discipline*, 177.

48. Robert Berkhofer, *Beyond the Great Story: History as Text and Discourse* (Princeton, NJ: Princeton University Press, 1995), 56.

49. Michel-Rolph Trouillot, *Silencing the Past: Power and the Production of History* (Boston: Beacon Press, 1995), 73.

50. Berkhofer, *Beyond the Great Story: History as Text and Discourse*.

51. Munslow, *Deconstructing History*, 124–125.

Chapter 2

'International Relations' in History

This chapter will focus on the manifestations of Eurocentrism within histo-riographical debates on the Cold War. The chapter is divided into three parts. The first part will discuss how historiography defines the parameters of the debate, especially with reference to the Cold War. The second part will focus on the main schools within the historiographical debate on the Cold War and discuss the borders they draw around the debate and the manifestations of Eurocentric assumptions within them. The third part will focus on writings of Turkish foreign policy and manifestations of Eurocentrism within the charac-terizations and conceptualizations on the Cold War.

The aim of this chapter is to underline the different ways in which Euro-centrism manifests itself in and through disciplines. The writing and making of history and the borders around historiographical debates establish a terrain upon which discussions, debates and disagreements can take place. As such, historiographical debates function to create the subject of inquiry. The Euro-centrism that manifests itself is primarily historical in the sense that 'world politics is taken to be happening almost exclusively in Europe, or latterly in the Northern hemisphere' and the entry of the Third World into debates 'is derivative of European developments and driven by great-power competition and the diffusion of European ideas and institutions'.[1] Nonetheless, it should be underlined that the writings and makings of the historiographical debate also function to delimit the possible and impossible.[2] Furthermore, the char-acterizations and framings of who is included and the reasons behind such inclusions and exclusions also contain within themselves culturalist manifes-tations. As such, even though the main focus is in and through history, the dif-ferent manifestations of Eurocentrism can be seen at work interdependently and simultaneously.

HISTORIOGRAPHICAL OPERATIONS[3]

This section will focus on the way in which the 'writing' and the 'making' of the Cold War as a historiographical terrain configured events, accorded different degrees of importance to certain actors and structured the narrative. The Cold War is one of the main examples of the 'Eurocentric historiographical geographies and periodisations' within 'common narratives of world history' that work to make the international intelligible.[4] As such, the way in which historiographical debates formulate the borders around events works to 'make' the possible histories that can be written on it.

Rigney discusses the preconfigured nature of 'received events' with respect to the French Revolution as follows:

> It is a 'site to be visited' or, if the nominal reference is to be expanded into a narrative account, it is a pre-arranged itinerary marking out the recommended scenic route (and the beaten track) from one major point of interest to the next – the Jeu de Paume (20 June 1789); the Taking of Bastille (14 July 1789); the abolition of feudal privileges (4 August 1789); the women at Versailles (5–6 October 1789); the Flight to Varennes (20–22 June 1791); the crowd's invasion of Tuileries (20 June 1792); the Storming of the Tuileries on 10 August 1792; the execution of Louis XVI (21 January 1793); and so on through the fall of the Girondins (2 June 1793), the *Terreur,* the trial and execution of Danton (13–16 Germinal *an* 11, 2–5 April 1794), and the fall of Robespierre on 9 Thermidor *an* 11 (27 July 1794).[5]

Thus, despite all the different ways in which the French Revolution might be narrated and differences 'in the degree of detail with which they treat particular episodes and in the particular links they establish between them, each one is structured around these canonical events, these areas of common historical account'.[6] The discussion around the French Revolution and the main stopping points in order to tell its story is demonstrative of 'Eurocentric historical geographies and periodisations'. The Haitian Revolution and its impact on the French Revolution becomes absent within the imaginations of the geographies and periodizations. As C.L.R James observes, 'Slave-trade and slavery were the economic basis of the French Revolution' and these forces 'linked San Domingo to the economic destiny of three continents and the social and political conflicts of that pregnant age'.[7] As such, the periodizations and geographies through which they are imagined are 'abstractions' that continue to be reproduced in International Relations (IR) discourse and are 'never innocent of power: the precise strategies and methods of abstraction in each instance decide what aspects of a limitless reality are brought into sharp focus and what aspects are, literally left out of the picture'.[8] As such, the Cold

War is one of the abstractions used within IR literature to simplify and explain international relations.[9]

The frame of the Cold War is the terrain upon which the historian navigates, and the different accounts of the Cold War(s) are mainly based upon the prioritization of events and different actors. Different itineraries might be followed, but the main sites to be visited are already inscribed into the very concept of the Cold War. Thus, one stops by Yalta, Potsdam, Poland, events in Eastern Europe in general, Turkey, Marshall Plan and Truman Doctrine. Yet, the time one spends in each stop differs according to the narrative configuration of the writer. As such, the master event and the narrative schema are already preconfigured when discussing the Cold War. It is within this schema that the historiographical operation takes place. The particular frames employed, the degrees of importance accorded to an event, how an 'event' is constituted as an event and the degrees of silence will determine the form of the content. As such, 'The commonplace of the revolutionary ship provides each writer with an empty frame or narrative grid, which can be filled in by different actors, depending on the particular configuration of the Revolution: the significant roles are already marked out, the historian only has to give them a figurative manifestation'.[10]

The Cold War serves to enable certain actions over others and prioritize certain actors over others. The main narrative terrain upon which the Cold War is built is Eurocentric, and 'the art of understanding a historical period exclusively through the Western experience of that period partakes in the same hegemonic Euro-Americanism that defined the conflict itself, privileging a limited range of subjectivities and relegating all others to insignificance'.[11] In that sense, the Cold War story is reflective of the subjectivities and priorities of a Eurocentric conceptualization of world politics. The naming, writing and making of the Cuban Missile Crisis is demonstrative of this point whereby the naming, writing and making of events could be different from the Cuban and Soviet perspectives.[12] For the Cubans the crisis was the October Crisis and for the Soviets the Caribbean crisis, both characterizations implying different geographical and historical imaginations. The Cuban perspective is invisible from the story of Cuban Missile Crisis and, as such, its writing and making ends up being not 'about Cuba or Cubans' but rather 'about the United States and the Soviet Union'.[13] The Cold War is a specific construction of a crisis serving a specific purpose with respect to the narrative of the US foreign policy and the international system.

The next two sections will thus focus on the 'writing' and 'making' of the Cold War and the ways in which the historiographical operations reproduced 'Eurocentric historiographical geographies and periodizations' not only in and between disciplines but also in and between different geopolitical contexts.

COLD WAR HISTORIOGRAPHY

This section focusing on the historiography of the Cold War is divided according to traditional divisions of Cold War historiographical schools.[14] Thus, 'because the character of historical interpretation resides in its narrative structure, historical knowledge is generated by constant debates between narratives (interpretations) rather than the primeval, unscripted and uncontextualized traces of the past'.[15] These schools look at the same period, but they analyse different actors, forces and events with differing perspectives, leading to incongruence among them. As Munslow states:

> Every historical interpretation is just one more in a long chain of interpretations, each one usually claiming to be closer to the reality of the past, but each one merely another reinscription of the same events, with each successive description being the product of the historian's imposition at the levels of the trope, emplotment, argument and ideology.[16]

As such, the differing schools all claim to represent the 'truth' and the 'past as it really happened', yet all of them employ discourses, ideological characterizations and theoretical generalities on the stories they tell. Therefore, the aim is not to present an exhaustive literature review but discuss the ways of speaking about the Cold War prevalent in the literature, to underline the historical interpretations, inscriptions of events, privileging of actors and configuration of the narrative terrain.

TRADITIONALISTS

The 'traditionalist' school is based on common conceptions of history, the United States and the Soviet Union. First, the traditionalist account presents a normative account of events based on explicit delineations of good and evil, moral and immoral and right and wrong. Secondly, the narrative fits into the general understanding of United States foreign policy whereby the isolationist, anti-imperialist and idealistic United States is pulled into European affairs in order to protect the world against the Soviet menace. As Hurst states: 'Traditionalism is better understood as an extension of the prevailing pre-Second World War historiography of US foreign diplomacy. That historiography was remarkably consensual and at the heat of that consensus was a celebratory, even triumphalist, interpretation of American foreign policy to that point'.[17]

The 'traditionalist' school has three main characteristics that need to be underlined. First, traditionalist accounts concentrate mainly on the decision makers of the time and their motivations, specifically the executive branch. The social, economic and cultural forces that defined the society, the institutions and the decision makers are largely ignored, as well as the structure of the international system. Secondly, US foreign policy is narrated as being passive until it is called upon to defend freedom and democracy. Hence, the United States is presented as reacting to events that occur in Europe and Asia rather than being an integral player. This presentation absolves the United States from any agency in creating the situations and crises of the post Second World War period. This leads to the third characteristic: the Soviet Union was responsible for the onset of the Cold War. Once the United States is narrated into the story as a passive actor that does not play an active role in the shaping of events, the Soviet Union becomes the state with all agency and active pursuit of goals is attributed to, thus making it responsible for igniting crises and conflicts where none would have existed otherwise.

Herbert Feis,[18] in his book *From Trust to Terror: The Onset of the Cold War, 1945–1950*, is representative of the traditionalist school. His presentation of events follows the conventional US foreign policy interpretation. Feis concentrates on Poland as being the evidence of Soviet intentions in a larger scale. He states that 'of all the ploys by which the Soviet Government brought its neighbours into subjection, Stalin's distortion of promises given regarding Poland was to hurt the most'.[19] This statement brings forward the assumption that guides Feis's study – that Britain and the United States were guided by benign motivations based on moralistic ideals, whereas the Soviet Union used 'ploys' and 'distortions' to bring Poland into 'subjection'. This narrative presents the United States as a bystander and not as a participant in the events that occurred; the Soviet Union, on the other hand, alters agreements and subjugates states. This is further evident in Feis's study when he states that 'Truman and his advisers sought settlements which corresponded to principles and aims that soared beyond the ordinary satisfactions and rewards of victory. They wanted to transmute the wartime alliance with the Russians into a lasting working accord for peace'.[20] This statement describing the Potsdam conference presents the United States as the selfless country that only aimed to cooperate; no other purpose, interest or goal is attributed to the United States. Feis states that 'while the United States ... was coming to the support of the Greek and Turkish governments, the Communists, Russian and local, expelled from power all political leaders in Hungary, Romania and Bulgaria whom they thought unfriendly'.[21] The differences in the characterization of actions are evident in this statement. In this reading, the United States 'comes to the support' of Greek and Turkish governments, whereas the Soviet Union 'expels from power' unfriendly leaders. With respect to the Potsdam meeting and the Soviet demands for access to the Straits, Feis presents the United States as attempting to placate the Soviets in the spirit of cooperation when

he states, 'The American Government, however, had tried to satisfy the reasonable element in Soviet aspirations – that it be assured of unhindered and
secure access through the Dardanelles to the Mediterranean and the seas and
lands'.[22] Thus, the United States tried to concede the 'reasonable elements'
and salvage cooperation. In sum, Feis's narrative presents a traditional story
of US foreign relations and embeds the Cold War as the latest stage of the
United States being called upon to restore peace in Europe. As a consequence, the United States is an actor that reacts to the situation rather than
one that plays an active role in creating it.

Louis J. Halle's book *Cold War as History* represents the second strand in
the traditionalist school. Halle argues that 'the gigantic power of Russia had
been contained or balanced' but 'what the situation of Europe represented, in
the years from 1945 to 1947, was a crisis in the balance of power'.[23] According to this narrative, the Cold War grew out of a vacuum in the balance of
power after the Second World War. Presenting an analysis of European history, Halle states, 'Since the end of the eighteenth century four great wars had
been fought to maintain or resolve the European balance of power. The fourth
was the Cold War, which began almost immediately after World War II'.[24]
This narrative situates the Cold War at the centre of the story whereby it is
the culmination of a specific understanding of European history. This puts
the Cold War at the end of a continuous line of events going back to the
eighteenth century, thus making it part of the linear story of power politics
and balance of power. By locating the sources of the Cold War in balance
of power, Halle proceeds to explain history of US foreign relations in a
traditionalist manner by stating that 'the American people, shaped by their
long-tradition, could not accept considerations of power politics as reasons
for going to war'; hence, they always looked for moral justifications. Even
though Halle characterizes US foreign relations as based upon isolationism
and moralism in tandem with the traditionalist perspective, he categorizes
this tendency as being naïve. He states: 'In 1917–1918, the United States,
morally and psychologically unequipped to do so, came into the war at the
eleventh hour, to restore the balance of power, while pretending that it was
doing something altogether different and nobler'.[25] Thus, US foreign policy
actions were always reticent towards power politics, whether after the First
World War or during the Second World War, and 'the lesson would finally be
learned only in 1947, when at last the United States, now grim and realistic,
would abandon its isolationist policy and all its outworn traditions in order to
meet the challenge of Stalin's Russia'.[26]

According to Halle, the roots of the Cold War could also be found in the
unrealistic policies of the United States. An example he provides is the policy
of insisting on the 'unconditional surrender' of Germany – he contends that
the trajectory of events could have been different if only the United States
had concluded a peace treaty with Germany under a new government and

ensured the establishment of a balance of power. He argues, 'The decision to eliminate German power from Europe, rather than make such a peace, is what laid the foundations of the Cold War'.[27] The division of Europe is attributed solely to the Soviet Union. Halle discusses the Marshall Plan as a vehicle to 'rescue' Europe and states that 'the Marshall proposal, and its eager acceptance in London and Paris, confronted Moscow with the final decision whether to join the West or to fight it'.[28] Soviet Union's negative response meant that 'Europe was finally divided'.[29] The Marshall Plan, in itself, is not seen as an active foreign policy endeavour that prompted a response from the Soviet Union, but rather the Soviet Union becomes the actor that 'divides' Europe by responding to the Marshall Plan. On the question of inevitability, Halle's stance is that 'the range of choice was small, the element of predetermination large'.[30] It was in the nature of the Soviet Union to act according to power politics, especially since the balance of power was not restored immediately after the war. The only logical deduction within this narrative is for the United States to restore the balance of power and contain the Soviet Union. According to Halle, 'The continuing expansion of Russia at the end of World War II alarmed the Western nations, impelling them to draw together for a common resistance. So, the retirement of the United States into its own hemisphere, which had just begun, was halted and reversed'.[31] The United States was inclined to return to its isolationist ways after the war and only reversed that policy once it comprehended the expansionist 'designs' of the Soviet Union. Thus, 'when the West rallied under American leadership to halt that expansion it was acting in its own legitimate defence rather than in a spirit of aggression'.[32]

To conclude, traditionalist accounts configure the events of the Cold War in such a way that situates Poland and Eastern Europe as the catalysis of the 'origins'. Privileging the events in Eastern Europe ascribes agency to the Soviet Union as the actor that was in the offensive. Furthermore, the story of the US foreign policy is depicted in a traditionalist fashion. The US foreign policy is configured to underline the naiveté and isolationism of the United States, and it is in an effort to restore the balance of power in Europe that the United States involves itself in European affairs. This narrative fits into a traditional narrative of European history whereby the developments from the eighteenth century onwards can be told in a linear manner as progressing towards US hegemony in order to solve the issue of balance of power within the international system.

REVISIONISTS

Revisionists are not a unified school, but there are certain characteristics that are shared by its representatives. First, revisionist works focus on the centrality of economic factors in determining US foreign policy. Secondly, contrary to traditional accounts of Cold War history, the US foreign policy is not characterized as isolationist or idealist but rather as expansionist. Thirdly, whereas traditionalists presented the United States as a passive actor, revisionists characterize it as playing an active role in shaping the circumstances of the post-Second World War international system. Fourthly, these works are united in their criticism of the US foreign policy. Fifthly, revisionism inverts the traditionalist argument as it locates the responsibility for the Cold War mainly with the United States.

William A. Williams is one of the best-known revisionists, and in his work *The Tragedy of American Diplomacy* he presents a narrative that challenges not only the traditional account of the Cold War but also US foreign policy in general. According to Williams, the origins of the Cold War can be found in the contradictions existing within US foreign policy – in other words, in the 'conflict within and between America's ideas and practice'.[33] Thus, contrary to the traditionalist argument, the reason for the onset of the Cold War can be found in US actions, which are not understood to be passive, but rather active and interventionist – in other words, the United States was an actor actively involved in shaping events. Furthermore, he does not concentrate solely on the post-Second World War period but presents a linear analysis of US foreign policy, locating the roots of the contradictions that led to the Cold War in the past. In the 1890s, during the economic crisis, 'when Americans *thought* that the frontier was gone, they advanced and accepted the argument that new expansion was the best, if not the only, way to sustain their freedom and prosperity'.[34] Hence, 'in response to the crisis of the 1890s, Americans developed a broad consensus in favour of an expansionist foreign policy as a solution to their existing troubles and as a way to prevent future difficulties'.[35] Williams argues that Spanish–American war was mainly motivated by these considerations, after which, with the open-door policy, the aim became 'to establish the conditions under which America's preponderant economic power would extend the American system throughout the world without the embarrassment and inefficiency of traditional colonialism'.[36] According to Williams, 'When combined with the ideology of an industrial Manifest Destiny, the history of the Open Door Notes became the history of US foreign relations from 1900 to 1958'.[37] This narrative present US foreign policy as a linear story of economic expansion and engulfs the Cold War into the story, making it yet another expression of US foreign policy objectives.

As such, the revisionist perspective also presents a linear story much like the traditionalists. Thus, even though the root causes of US foreign policymaking is inverted and an alternative interpretation is narrated, the narrative itself remains Western-centric in that the main catalyst for explaining world politics remains the West. Contrary to the traditionalists who had presented a passive United States, the revisionist perspective presents a passive Soviet Union. The Soviet Union becomes the actor who has to react to the dynamic and aggressive foreign policy pursued by the United States. The 'Russian expansion' into Eastern Europe is narrated within this perspective of ensuring the continuance of open-door policy whereby 'such protests were not prompted by the fear that Russia was about to overwhelm Europe or the world in general, but rather by the traditional outlook of the open door and the specific desire to get the Russians out of Eastern Europe'.[38] The narrative presented by Williams is the story of the open-door policy adopted by the US policymakers coupled with their belief in Manifest Destiny induced them to act in a manner that limited the choices available to the Soviet Union.

Both traditionalism and revisionism present the United States and the Soviet Union as one-dimensional actors with monocausal interests. As a consequence, the comprehension of the Cold War becomes confined to either/or dichotomies influenced by ideological interpretations of US foreign policy. Furthermore, they both work within the main contours defined by the Eurocentric narrative. The Cold War is about what it means for US foreign policy: Is it economically expansionist or is it a naïve state that was called upon a moral mission? The narrative configurations within the story of the Cold War change depending on which interpretation of US foreign policy is adopted. As such, the terrain of the Cold War does not change.

POST-REVISIONIST

John Lewis Gaddis in his seminal work *The United States and the Origins of the Cold War*[39] presents a narrative that aims to balance the traditionalist and revisionist interpretations of the origins of the Cold War even though his interpretations remain closer to that of traditionalists than revisionists. On the issue of inevitability and the assigning of blame for the origins of the Cold War, Gaddis argues, 'The power vacuum in central Europe caused by Germany's collapse made a Russian-American confrontation likely, it did not make it inevitable'.[40] Gaddis puts the impending US–Russian rivalry in the context of the nature of the international system. The systemic analysis is present in this account whereby the power vacuum created after the Second World leaves the two great powers in a security dilemma, and the story of the Cold War is about the restoration of balance of power and solving the security dilemma. According to this narrative, the 'Cold War grew out of a complicated interaction of external and internal developments inside both the United States and the Soviet Union'.[41] The external situation was the structural condition of the international system that left the two great powers, the Soviet Union and the United States, facing each other. This narrative configuration continues in the trajectory of the 'traditionalist' and 'revisionist' analysis in the privileging of a specific understanding of European balance of power story.

Melvyn P. Leffler's[42] *Preponderance of Power* diverges with Gaddis's account on several points, as will be discussed. Leffler concentrates on concepts such as correlations of power, national security and geopolitics to explain the actions of the United States. Thus, according to Leffler,

> Neither the Americans, nor the Soviets sought to harm the other in 1945. But each side, in pursuit of its security interests, took steps that aroused the other's apprehensions. Moreover, the protests that each country's actions evoked from the other fuelled the cycle of distrust as neither could comprehend the fears of the other, perceiving its own actions as defensive. Herein rests the classic security dilemma.[43]

For Leffler, the main roots of the Cold War can be located in the security dilemma created by the structure of the international system. Within that system, 'US officials defined their national security in terms of correlations of power. US officials believed that they had to relieve the problems besetting the industrial democracies of Western Europe, integrate former enemies like Germany and Japan into the international economy. … If they failed in these tasks, the correlation of power in the international system would be transformed. The Soviet Union would grow stronger, the United States weaker'.[44] Further, he states that 'their overriding priority was to prevent a totalitarian adversary from conquering or assimilating the resources of Europe and Asia and using them to wage war against the United States, as the Axis powers had done during World War II'.[45] Leffler further stressed that 'the most important National Security Council (NSC) papers of the Truman administration incorporated a geostrategic vision. National security was interpreted in terms of correlations of power. Power was defined in terms of the control of resources, industrial infrastructure and overseas bases'.[46] It is thus geopolitical considerations and the security dilemma within the United States and the Soviet Union that constitute the underlying causes of the Cold War. Despite the systemic determinants, Leffler does ascribe agency to the actors for even though the security dilemma existed ever since the end of the Second World War, it took time for the Cold War to get started. According to Leffler, Cold War began in 1946 'when US officials defined the Soviet union as the enemy', and rather 'than focus on the popular desire for reform and recovery throughout Europe, rather than emphasize the indigenous source of civil strife in Asia, and rather than identifying with revolutionary nationalism in the Third World, they latched onto an interpretation of international developments that placed blame and responsibility on the Kremlin'.[47] In conclusion, the narrative configurations of the events altered and different priorities were ascribed to actors, yet the main Eurocentric conceptualization of world politics remained. It was the story of a European balance of power that needed to be maintained and the power vacuum that appeared after the Second World War, leaving two super-powers face to face. To summarize:

> The Cold War was the legacy of World War II. That conflict deranged the international system, altered the balance of power in Europe, shattered colonial empires, restructured economic and social arrangements within nations and bequeathed a legacy of fear that preordained a period of unusual anxiety and tension.[48]

PERICENTRISTS

Towards the end of the 1980s, the post-revisionist school led the way for the pericentrist school. The pericentrist school appeared towards the 'end', insert-ing into the literature the British story.[49] Deighton inserts Great Britain into the narrative about the origins and underlines that 'British decision-makers assessed early on that they would have to base postwar foreign policy both on the threat from Communist ideology and on the consequences of the arrival of the Soviet Union as the new great power on the world stage'.[50] In line with the post-revisionist and systemic explanations, Deighton underlines that the main priority was not communism or the Soviet Union but 'to maintain Britain's place as a major global and imperial power in a rapidly changing period of fresh ideological and power political challenges'.[51] Hence, she argues 'that this priority would still have existed in Britain even if the Soviet Union had withdrawn from active international politics'.[52]

Vojtech Mastny's book *The Cold War and Soviet Insecurity* is both neo-traditionalist and pericentrist. Mastny focuses on the Russian story and the reasons behind the policies they pursued and adopted. According to Mastny, Stalin's motivation was the attainment of security, and 'he tried to accomplish what he wanted with rather than against his powerful Western allies, whose support, or at least acquiescence, he deemed indispensable for achieving the kind of security he craved'.[53] Mastny argued that 'what went wrong at Yalta was the way how the participants badly misjudged each other's intentions'.[54] Mastny locates the origins of the Cold War within the Soviet Union and argues that 'the roots of the conflict were domestic and ideological. Rather than sharing with his people relief at the end of their wartime suffering, Stalin saw a threat to his tyranny in their expectations of a better life. He needed to justify it by convincing them that they remained surrounded by enemies'.[55] Despite the restraints showed at times in an effort to maintain the alliance, the Cold War was still inevitable because the Soviet Union necessitated an enemy. Mastny's narrative presents a story in which the Cold War grows out of the sense of insecurity felt by Soviet leaders, as a consequence of which they took 'greater risks whenever they saw the correlation of forces turning in their favour. In estimating their own strengths and the weaknesses of their adversaries, they were prone to miscalculation. They were enhanced by their ideological preconceptions, which postulated the ultimate victory of their system'.[56] In addition to arguing that the Soviet search for security was rooted in domestic factors, Mastny also stresses that it was the changing balance of power in the international system that caused the Soviet system to attempt to expand into areas such as Turkey and Iran.

Thus, adding Britain into the narrative does not alter the main assumptions of the story but adds another actor into the equation. The story of the origins remains the same. Since the end, the story has been extended to Africa, Asia, Middle East and Eastern Europe.[57] Yet, pericentrism does not constitute a separate school on the origins of the Cold War because even though the focus shifts the central parameters of the narrative schema are reproduced for other stories. There are many Cold War(s) within the Cold War schema, but the structure of the story and the configurations, prioritizations and what counts as 'events' do not alter.

REPRODUCING THE 'COLD WAR'

The manifestations of Eurocentrism in and through disciplines do not make up just the story of the scholarship of the 'centre'; they are also seen in the scholarship of the 'periphery'. To explain this, take the example of Turkey. 'Turkey' is generally seen as inhabiting an 'in-between' space, as an actor bridging the East and the West (although the latter in its discussions about 'Turkey' continues to erect boundaries). 'Turkey' in that sense is an interesting case for reflecting on a variety of anxieties[58] with respect to locating the 'non-West'.

FOREIGN POLICY NARRATIVES

The two texts that will be in focus in this section are two narratives of Turkish foreign policy that are premised upon critical international relations defined broadly.

Bozdağlıoğlu in *Turkish foreign policy and Turkish identity* adopts a constructivist approach to analysing Turkish foreign policy. He argues that Turkey 'constitutes a unique case study to assess the validity of the constructivist perspective', since 'Turkey holds a special place in the international system' because 'it is on the very borderlines between "North versus South" and "East versus West" and among different civilizations: the Muslim, Middle Eastern and the Western'.[59] Such a narrative reinforces Turkey's exceptionalism narrative because of its geopolitical location.[60] The aim of the narrative, as stated, is to uncover why Turkey, 'throughout its history, fully identified itself with the West'.[61] This approach attempts to question the basis of the Turkish identity that was constructed after the Turkish War of Independence based on a specific understanding of modernization that 'was a project of embracing and internalizing all the cultural dimensions that made Europe modern'.[62] It is within this framework that Bozdağlıoğlu discusses relations with the United States and the Cold War by stating that 'after Atatürk's death in 1939, his successors took further steps to make Turkey an actual ally of the West. This process began in 1939 with the tripartite agreement between Turkey, Britain and France, developed further after World War II when Turkey joined NATO, the Council of Europe and other Western organizations'.[63] Hence, the events that led to the onset of the Cold War and Turkey's alliances are seen to be the natural expressions of the Westernization project that Turkey had embarked upon at its inception. Furthermore, he argues that Turkey's 'alliance' continued even when its 'national interests' were perceived to be at stake and 'uncompromising devotion to the West and Western institutions persisted even when the advantages and disadvantages of these institutions to Turkey's national interest were seriously questioned in the country'.[64]

According to this narrative, Turkey's national identity is predicated on an understanding of modernization interchangeably linked to Westernization and its foreign policy is a manifestation of this will to emulate and integrate with the 'West'. Such a narrative ascribes continuity to Turkish foreign policymaking whereby the aims and motivations have not altered, and rather than explain how such an identity has been maintained for over half a century, it is taken as a constant that cannot be challenged. The Cold War itself becomes a manifestation of a foreign policy orientation rooted in modernization. Furthermore, the Cold War becomes a vehicle for Turkey's acceptance by the West whereby 'it was in the context of the Cold War that Turkey was able to establish close relations with the West'.[65] As a consequence, Turkey's role as a 'Western' state is questioned once the Cold War ends both internally and externally. Bozdağlıoğlu ascribes to a traditionalist narrative of Cold War periodization whereby the period of the Cold War as accepted, 1945–1990, is a period where the main assumptions of westernization, modernization and alliance with the United States are not radically questioned.

Bozdağlıoğlu's analysis of Turkish foreign policy can be characterized as a 'genealogy of continuity' whereby he brings forward the discourse of westernization, modernization and Turkey's 'exceptional' status in the international system as a country that inhabits a space at the intersection of North and South and East and West divisions. This narrative obscures the ruptures, divisions and alternatives that existed within the time frame under consideration and presents a linear story of Turkey's alliance with the West. The Cold War is presented as a period where westernization, Turkey's orientations and its motivations are hardly criticized. The same is valid for when Bozdağlıoğlu discusses how westernization became the dominant identifier for Turkey, he does not discuss the alternatives of this identifier and whether or not the alternatives being silenced meant their non-existence or their being pushed to the fringes. Furthermore, Bozdağlıoğlu overlooks how Turkey negotiated '"difference" in the face of a European/International Society that was ambivalent towards its difference'.[66]

Bostanoğlu presents an analysis of Turkish foreign policy and Turkey–US relations based on critical international theory mainly derived from the works of Robert Cox in *The Politics of Turkey-US Relations*. She adopts Cox's definition of hegemony as 'a value system that permeates the entire international system' and is maintained by 'legitimating practices and ideologies'.[67] According to Bostanoğlu, post-Second World War period can be best comprehended as the establishment of hegemony by the United States whereby the 'administration had determined that American aims for a global role were threatened and declared the Soviets and communist parties who started expansionist policies in Eastern Europe as enemies of humanity'.[68] It was not communism *per se* that was their concern, but 'they made war with communism the centre of US policies in order to get what they wanted from Congress and the allies'.[69] With respect to the Truman Doctrine, Bostanoğlu remarks that 'even though the Truman Doctrine was about containing the Soviet Union, economic considerations also played a role'.[70]

With respect to Turkey, Bostanoğlu states, 'In this period, Turkey assumed a pivotal role in US policy to contain the Soviet Union, and assumed her role in US hegemonic system with the Truman doctrine and the Marshall Plan'.[71] Thus, within the hegemonic system that the United States was establishing, Turkey was a willing participant because 'Turkey identified her interests with the Cold War and with being on the US camp. The basis of her diplomacy from the Truman Doctrine to participating in the Korean War, from recognizing Israel to entering NATO, was a willingness to demonstrate her loyalty to the US alliance system'.[72] One of the main reasons for this compulsion to side with the West was 'the internal desire Turkey had for development and the need for American aid to realize this played a pivotal role in Ankara willingly entering the international system the US created and led'.[73] As such, Bostanoğlu argues, 'Turkey being situated within the American hegemony was due to Turkish foreign policy being guided by a realist search for security'.[74] Bostanoğlu considers the post-Second World War alignment of Turkey inevitable because of the manner in which Turkey in analysing the international system in realist fashion defined the Cold War and its national interests in a certain manner. Yet, Bostanoğlu does not discuss how this definition took place and why the 'realist' perspective became dominant rather than other ways of perceiving the international system at the time or whether or not there were alternatives.

RELATIONS WITH THE UNITED STATES

George McGhee, in *The-US-Turkish-NATO-Middle East Connection: How the Truman Doctrine and Turkey's NATO Entry Contained the Soviets*, as the title suggests, concentrates on the regional aspects and portrays Turkey's alliance with the United States as a successful policy pursued by US foreign policy decision makers. He states that 'when the United States decided in 1947 to provide Turkey with massive military assistance under the Truman Doctrine and in the early 1950s to help Turkey gain admission to the NATO alliance, the door to a Soviet invasion of the Middle East was slammed shut'.[75] Hence, the Truman Doctrine is characterized as not only aiding Turkey in the face of Soviet expansionism but also preventing Soviet expansion into the Near East and Middle East. Furthermore, McGhee argues, 'Turkey's decision to join NATO and the West was not, I believe, the result of a temporary convenience or opportunism. It can best be described as the meeting of historical trends that were operating in both Turkey and the West'.[76] The narrative of westernization and modernization is present in McGhee's account whereby the actions and choices made by Turkey were also about fulfilling the project of westernization which the alliance with the 'West' was an important part of.

McGhee presents a traditionalist Cold War explanation whereby he states that 'the West, particularly the United States, recognized after the last war the aggressive and expansionist nature of Soviet communism and determined to protect themselves and the free world against it'.[77] Hence, the United States reacted towards Soviet aggressiveness and expansionism in order to protect itself and the free world. Within this narrative, the Cold War was caused by Soviet actions whereby the Truman Doctrine was a policy that succeeded in preventing it. Furthermore, according to this narrative, Turkey was included within the Truman Doctrine because 'failure to aid Greece could convince the Turks that it would be less dangerous to yield to Soviet pressures, even without a direct military threat, than to try to resist'.[78] McGhee ascribes to the traditional US foreign policy narrative and attempts to situate Turkey within that story. As such, it is a reproduction of the Western-centric narratives of the international system.

Oral Sander's *Turkish-American Relation 1947–1964* concentrates on the bilateral relations. Sander argues that the 'Truman Doctrine was the

first indicator after the Second World War between Western countries who
wanted to continue a system that was destroyed 25 years ago and the Soviet
Union that had no allegiance to the system and interpreted it as being against
themselves'.[79] Hence, the definition of the Cold War presents a perspective
more akin to the revisionist school in Cold War historiography. Rather than
defining America as reacting to Soviet aggressiveness, the conflict is narrated as emanating from attempts and differences in defining the post-Second
World War international system. He argues that the aim of the United States
was to 'contain Soviet expansionism where ever in the world and to ensure
American economic and political expansion'; hence, 'the Truman Doctrine
and Marshall Plan ended the transitory phase of the "Cold War"'.[80] The Cold
War is presented as having been caused by US actions and policies such as
the Truman Doctrine and Marshall Plan that aimed to expand US economic
interests. The reasons for Turkish foreign policy decision-making and alliance with the United States is listed as 'Soviet threat against Turkey after the
Second World War, the economic aid necessary for Turkey to realize development and westernization efforts that started with Ataturk'.[81] Hence, according
to Sander, 'Moscow's threat continued in 1947 and Turkish policy-makers
believed that safety against the Soviet Union could only be maintained by
Western alliance'.[82]

Türkkaya Ataöv in *NATO and Turkey* argues, 'Under the cover of the "Cold
War" epitaph, the United States is endeavouring to subdue all her allies and
prevent them from pursuing an independent foreign and domestic foreign
policy. The *sine qua non* of this subordination is the acceptance of the main
cold war issues, notably the "communist menace"'.[83] Ataöv presents a narrative in revisionist fashion by arguing that

> the U.S. pretended that the world's difficulties were due to the Soviet Union, and
> its 'agents' or 'fellow-travellers'. It seldom considered whether or not most of it
> was its own Open Door Policy. A cardinal truth of our century is that American
> leadership is still enhancing the traditional objective of the 1890s. For decades
> nothing satisfied the U.S. but free access to foreign markets. Expansion over-
> seas was thought of as the solution to the recurring economic crisis. Production
> had increased so enormously that new markers were needed to dispose of the
> surplus. The Open Door Policy has enabled the U.S. to 'stabilize' the world in
> favour of the American metropolis and establish a new empire.[84]

With respect to Turkey, Ataöv argues, 'The ruling circles of Turkey, having
failed to develop the country, tied their hopes to the capitalist classes in the
West. From the point of view of the existing social classes in Turkey, the
Second world War stimulated the Turkish bourgeoisie and helped it to be
stronger' whereby 'it was under these circumstances that the two leftist parties were brought to the court, the newly-formed unions were closed down,

a leftwing printing press was smashed after mob attack encouraged and directed by the government'.[85] According to Ataöv's narrative, Turkey's alliance had already been decided because of the capitalist leanings of the state and the rising bourgeois class. As such, 'Even before the famous Soviet notes were submitted to Turkey, the country was ripe ... to take part in the Western world'.[86] The Soviet Union and the Soviet threat were used to make the alliance easier rather than being the reasons for it. Within this narrative, Turkey is not without alternative, but rather it willingly chooses to ally with the West. It does not ally with the West because of any external threat but because of the domestic alignment of forces that favour capitalism. Turkey's relations with the United States and narratives of it were conditioned by the manner in which the Turkish state identified itself.

COLD WAR

This section will focus on works that deal specifically with the Cold War as the focus of the story. Ayşegül Sever's book *Soğuk Savaş Kuşatmasinda Turkiye, Batı ve Orta Dogu* (Turkey, the West and the Middle East Within the Cold War Encirclement) is one of the few books that deals exclusively with the Cold War. Sever argues for adopting a post-revisionist posture by stating that 'Cold War years are no longer just focusing on the United States-Soviet Union struggle and as a consequence Great Britain's role in the birth and development of the Cold War is being stressed in many works'.[87] As such, she concentrates on the role of Great Britain specifically with respect to Turkey. Her narrative takes the story of Russian–Turkish relations back to the nineteenth century, stressing the continuity in Russian motivations when she argues that 'in the past the Russians, especially in the nineteenth century, would pressure the Ottomans whenever they felt powerful to establish control of the Straits'.[88] The narrative is based on continuing Russian aggressiveness and Turkish efforts to prevent Russian expansion towards Turkey and convince the allies of the urgency of the threat. She argues, 'The Turkish government had urged Washington to take a firm stance towards the Soviet Union by sending a series of reports ever since the end of the war'.[89] Furthermore, according to Sever's story, Great Britain realizes the threat and together with Turkey attempts to persuade the United States of its existence whereby 'England already had doubts after the war as it had during, about whether cooperation with the Soviets could be continued'.[90] Thus, 'In parallel with the Inönü administration the English government believed that Soviet demands towards Turkey could not be accepted and would violate post-war international peace efforts'.[91] According to this, the United States realized the danger posed by the Soviet Union, of which Turkey and Great Britain had been aware, with time. She argues, 'By 1946, United States had realized that Soviet demands towards Turkey was an example of its expansionist policies and joined Great Britain'.[92] As such, despite claims of post-revisionism, the argument does resemble the traditionalist historiography whereby the United States realizes the Soviet expansionist aims and reacts to them.

Sever's book presents the process of the evolving Cold War, analysing the people, policies and the process involved, but her narrative also perpetuates some dominant narratives about Soviet relations with Turkey. Sever states, 'Turkey when faced with Soviet demands decided that they could no longer follow a policy of neutrality and that their future was with the West'.[93] Furthermore, the narrative ascribes to a 'traditional' interpretation of US foreign policy. The story presented can be considered as being pericentrist in that it aims to bring in Turkey to the story of the Cold War and to underline Turkey as one of the actors to convince the United States of the threat posed by the Soviet Union.

Ekavi Athanassopoulou's book, *Turkey: Anglo-American Security Interests, 1945–1952: The First Enlargement of NATO*, concentrates on the origins of the Cold War, specifically the process of Turkey joining NATO. The narrative is based more upon the events leading up to Turkey's membership of NATO and brings forth analysis of the main characters and events of the period under analysis, but Athanassopoulou, like Sever, does perpetuate dominant narratives about Turkish foreign policy. The account is one of a 'realistic' foreign policy whereby she argues that 'Turkish foreign policy remained consistent in what had always been a pragmatic orientation'.[94] Furthermore, she states that 'the pragmatic Turkish leaders never concealed their distrust of Moscow and their preference, should the question arise to side with the powers which were interested in guaranteeing the regional *status quo* and represented the western world into which Turkey wished to be integrated'.[95] This statement has two assumptions in line with the dominant narratives about Turkish foreign policy. First, the distrust towards Moscow had always existed, establishing a continuity between nineteenth-century Russia and the Soviet Union whereby the period of cooperation that started with the establishment of the Republic becomes a 'pragmatic' and 'realistic' policy. As such, Turkish alliance with the Soviet Union becomes one of convenience rather than one of genuine trust. This leads to the second assumption, which is that genuine trust existed towards the western powers with whom Turkey wished to integrate. The narrative of westernization and modernization and the aim of the Republic to become integrated with the West are present in the account. Turkey's aim from its establishment onwards was to achieve westernization and modernization, thus her 'natural allies' were the Western states and not the Soviet Union.

Athanassopoulou presents a traditionalist account of the Cold War when she argues that 'Washington's decision to resist any Soviet expansion in the eastern Mediterranean by building up Turkey's military strength', hence Washington becomes a passive actor realizing Soviet 'designs' after which it decides to prevent them. As a consequence, 'after its notes of 1946 Moscow did not resume its diplomatic pressure on Ankara. Thanks to the combined British-American support, the Turkish government found itself in a strong position regarding Stalin's designs'.[96] Thus, as with Sever, Athanassopoulou's narrative is a pericentrist account of the Cold War and the agency given to Turkey is one of an actor that demonstrates to the United States the importance of maintaining the balance of power. Accounts of the Cold War have adhered to traditionalist Cold War narratives with respect to the origins. The Soviet Union is narrated as being expansionist, whereas the United States is presented as being on the defensive. Furthermore, embedding Turkey into this narrative has been done in a way that reinforces the dominant narratives about Turkish foreign policy. The 'realist' and 'rational' choice of a westernizing and modernizing Turkish state was to ally itself against an expansionist Soviet Union.

CONCLUSION

The works discussed constitute the main pillars of the historiographical discourses on the Cold War and are also constitutive of Cold War narrative configurations. The double movement of the historiographical operation on the Cold War moves to create the 'Cold War', but it is also constituted and limited by the borders established during that operation.[97] The aim of the chapter has been to demonstrate the manifestations of Eurocentrism in and through disciplines and geopolitical contexts. This has been done through underlining the way the 'writing' and 'making' of the Cold War presents itself in historiographical debates. The Eurocentrism that manifests itself was primarily historical in the sense that it takes Europe and the West as the central subject of history and any other story that might exist as an offshoot of the European story. The borders of the historiographical debate 'write' and 'make' the Cold War. The chapter discussed how different perspectives on the Cold War may produce different histories of the Cold War without moving away from the historiographical terrain on which the West is the central subject of history.

NOTES

1. Barkawi and Laffey, 'The Postcolonial Moment in Security Studies', 334–335.
2. Trouillot, *Silencing the Past: Power and the Production of History.*
3. Certeau, *The Writing of History.*

4. Barkawi and Laffey, 'The Postcolonial Moment in Security Studies', 334.

5. Ann Rigney, *The Rhetoric of Historical Representation: Three Narrative Histories of the French Revolution* (Cambridge: Cambridge University Press, 2002), 37.

6. *The Rhetoric of Historical Representation: Three Narrative Histories of the French Revolution*.

7. C. L. R. James, *The Black Jacobins* (New York: The Dial Press, 1938), 47–55.

8. Krishna, 'Race, Amnesia, and the Education of International Relations', 403.

9. For works that have problematized the Cold War in IR literature, see: Cynthia Enloe, *The Morning After: Sexual Politics at the End of the Cold War* (Berkeley: University of California Press, 1993); Jutta Weldes et al., eds. *Cultures of Insecurity: States, Communities and the Production of Danger* (Minneapolis, MN: University of Minnesota Press, 1999); Jennifer Milliken, 'Intervention and Identity: Reconstructing the West in Korea', in *Cultures of Insecurity: States, Communities and the Production of Danger*, ed. Jutta Weldes, Mark Laffey, Hugh Gusterson, Raymond Duvall (Minneapolis, MN: University of Minnesota Press, 1999); Hugh Gusterson, 'Missing the End of the Cold War in International Security', in *Cultures of Insecurity: States, Communities and the Production of Danger*, ed. Jutta Weldes, et al. (Minneapolis, MN: University of Minnesota Press, 1999); Enloe, *The Morning After: Sexual Politics at the End of the Cold War*; Mark Laffey and Jutta Weldes, 'Decolonizing the Cuban Missile Crisis', *International Studies Quarterly* 52 (2008): 555–577; Richard Saull, 'Locating the Global South in the Theorisation of the Cold War: Capitalist Development, Social Revolution and Geopolitical Conflict', *Third World Quarterly* 26, no. March (2005): 253–280.

10. Rigney, *The Rhetoric of Historical Representation: Three Narrative Histories of the French Revolution*, 46.

11. Andrew Hammond, 'From Rhetoric to Rollback: Introductory Thoughts on Cold War Writing', in *Cold War Literature: Writing the Global Conflict*, ed. Andrew Hammond (New York and London: Routledge, 2006), 1.

12. Laffey and Weldes, 'Decolonizing the Cuban Missile Crisis'.

13. 'Decolonizing the Cuban Missile Crisis', 558.

14. It should be noted that the classical division of Cold War historiography, like the division of IR theory, is in many respects artificial and a tool in reproducing a certain narrative of the Cold War and the international system. It is employed here for reasons of simplification and with the aim to organize the works in a recognizable manner. Nevertheless, the constructed nature of the divisions and the manner in which they themselves are a part of the dominant narrative should not be overlooked.

15. Munslow, *Deconstructing History*, 173.

16. *Deconstructing History*, 35.

17. Steven Hurst, *Cold War US Foreign Policy: Key Perspectives* (Edinburgh: Edinburgh University Press, 2005), 26.

18. Herbert Feis, *From Trust to Terror: The Onset of the Cold War, 1945–1950* (New York: W.W. Norton, 1970).

19. *From Trust to Terror: The Onset of the Cold War, 1945–1950*, 23.

20. *From Trust to Terror: The Onset of the Cold Wa r, 1945–1950*, 43.

21. *From Trust to Terror: The Onset of the Cold War, 1945–1950*, 173–4.

22. *From Trust to Terror: The Onset of the Cold War, 1945–1950*, 179.

23. Louis Halle, *The Cold War as History* (London: Chatto and Windus, 1967), 2.

24. *The Cold War as History*, 2.

25. *The Cold War as History*, 26.

26. *The Cold War as History*, 26.

27. *The Cold War as History*, 36.

28. *The Cold War as History*, 130.

29. *The Cold War as History*, 135.

30. *The Cold War as History*, 76.

31. *The Cold War as History*, 145.

32. *The Cold War as History*, 416.

33. William Appelman Williams, *The Tragedy of American Diplomacy* (New York: Delta, 1962), 13.

34. *The Tragedy of American Diplomacy*, 26.

35. *The Tragedy of American Diplomacy*, 29.

36. *The Tragedy of American Diplomacy*, 37.

37. *The Tragedy of American Diplomacy*, 39–40.

38. *The Tragedy of American Diplomacy*, 165.

39. John Lewis Gaddis, *The United States and the Origins of the Cold War, 1941–1947* (New York: Columbia University Press, 1972).

40. *The United States and the Origins of the Cold War, 1941–1947*, 359.

41. *The United States and the Origins of the Cold War, 1941–1947*, 361.

42. For a more recent analysis of the Cold War by Melvyn P. Leffler, see: Melvyn P. Leffler, *For the Soul of Mankind: The United States, the Soviet Union, and the Cold War* (New York: Hill & Wang, 2007).

43. Melvyn P. Leffler, *A Preponderance of Power: National Security, the Truman Administration, and the Cold War* (Stanford: Stanford University Press, 1992), 99.

44. *A Preponderance of Power: National Security, the Truman Administration, and the Cold War*, 10.

45. 'The Emergence of an American Grand Strategy, 1945–1952', in *The Cambridge History of the Cold War*, ed. Melvyn P Leffler and Odd Arne Westad (Cambridge: Cambridge University Press, 2010), 77.

46. 'The Emergence of an American Grand Strategy, 1945–1952'.

47. *A Preponderance of Power: National Security, the Truman Administration, and the Cold War*, 100.

48. Leffler, *A Preponderance of Power*, 513.

49. Anne Deighton, 'Britain and the Cold War', in *The Cambridge History of the Cold War, Vol.1*, ed. Melvyn P. Leffler and Odd Arne Westad (Cambridge: Cambridge University Press, 2010).

50. 'Britain and the Cold War', 112.

51. 'Britain and the Cold War', 113.

52. 'Britain and the Cold War'.

53. Vojtech Mastny, *The Cold War and Soviet Insecurity: The Stalin Years* (New York: Oxford University Press, 1996), 21.

54. *The Cold War and Soviet Insecurity: The Stalin Years*, 22.

55. *The Cold War and Soviet Insecurity: The Stalin Years*, 24.

56. *The Cold War and Soviet Insecurity: The Stalin Years*, 191.

57. Sue Onslow, *Cold War in Southern Africa: White Power, Black Liberation* (London and New York: Routledge, 2009); Odd Arne Westad, *The Global Cold War: Third World Interventions and the Making of Our Times* (Cambridge: Cambridge University Press, 2005); Robert J. McMahon, *The Cold War on the Periphery: The United States, India, and Pakistan* (Columbia: Columbia University Press, 1994); Vesselin Dimitrov, *Stalin's Cold War: Soviet Foreign Policy, Democracy and Communism in Bulgaria, 1941–1948* (London: Palgrave Macmillan, 2007).

58. Bilgin and Ince, 'Security and Citizenship in the Global South: In/Securing Citizens in Early Republican Turkey (1923–1946)'; Bilgin and Bilgiç, 'Turkey and Eu/Rope: Discourses of Inspiration/Anxiety in Turkey's Foreign Policy'.

59. Yücel Bozdağlıoğlu, *Turkish Foreign Policy and Turkish Identity: A Constructivist Approach* (London: Routledge, 2004), 4.

60. Pınar Bilgin, 'Turkey's "Geopolitics Dogma"', in *The Return of Geopolitics in Europe? Social Mechanisms and Foreign Policy Identity Crises*, ed. Stefano Guzzini (Cambridge: Cambridge University Press, 2012).

61. Bozdağlıoğlu, *Turkish Foreign Policy and Turkish Identity: A Constructivist Approach*, 3.

62. *Turkish Foreign Policy and Turkish Identity: A Constructivist Approach*, 29.

63. *Turkish Foreign Policy and Turkish Identity: A Constructivist Approach*, 52.

64. *Turkish Foreign Policy and Turkish Identity: A Constructivist Approach*, 61.

65. *Turkish Foreign Policy and Turkish Identity: A Constructivist Approach*, 6.

66. Pınar Bilgin, 'Securing Turkey through Western-Oriented Foreign Policy', *New Perspectives on Turkey* 45, no. 2 (2009), 107. Also see, Bilgin, *The International in Security, Security in the International*.

67. Burcu Bostanoğlu, *Türkiye-Abd İlişkilerinin Politikası: Kuram Ve Siyaset* (Ankara: İmge Kitabevi, 1999), 190.

68. *Türkiye-Abd İlişkilerinin Politikası: Kuram Ve Siyaset*, 238.

69. *Türkiye-Abd İlişkilerinin Politikası: Kuram Ve Siyaset*, 238.

70. *Türkiye-Abd İlişkilerinin Politikası: Kuram Ve Siyaset*, 243.

71. *Türkiye-Abd İlişkilerinin Politikası: Kuram Ve Siyaset*, 331.

72. *Türkiye-Abd İlişkilerinin Politikası: Kuram Ve Siyaset*, 336.

73. *Türkiye-Abd İlişkilerinin Politikası: Kuram Ve Siyaset*, 332.

74. *Türkiye-Abd İlişkilerinin Politikası: Kuram Ve Siyaset*, 380.

75. George C. McGhee, *The US-Turkish-NATO Middle East Connection: How the Truman Doctrine and Turkey's NATO Entry Contained the Soviets* (Basingstoke: Macmillan, 1990), xii.

76. McGhee, *The US-Turkish-NATO Middle East Connection*, 9.

77. McGhee, *The US-Turkish-NATO Middle East Connection*, 9–10.

78. McGhee, *The US-Turkish-NATO Middle East Connection*, 21.

79. Oral Sander, *Türk-Amerikan Iliskileri, 1947–1964* (Ankara: A.U. Siyasal Bilgiler Fakültesi, 1979), 13.

80. Sander, *Türk-Amerikan Iliskileri*, 18.

81. Sander, *Türk-Amerikan Iliskileri*, 18.

82. Sander, *Türk-Amerikan Iliskileri*, 19.

83. Türkkaya Ataöv, *NATO and Turkey* (Ankara: Sevinç Print. House, 1970), 1.

84. *NATO and Turkey*, 5.

85. *NATO and Turkey*, 91.

86. *NATO and Turkey*, 92.

87. Ayseğül Sever, 'Soğuk Savaş Kuşatmasında Türkiye, Batı Ve Orta Doğu 1945–1958' (Istanbul: Boyut Kitapları, 1997), 12.

88. 'Soğuk Savaş Kuşatmasında Türkiye, Batı Ve Orta Doğu 1945–1958', 17.

89. 'Soğuk Savaş Kuşatmasında Türkiye, Batı Ve Orta Doğu 1945–1958', 26.

90. 'Soğuk Savaş Kuşatmasında Türkiye, Batı Ve Orta Doğu 1945–1958', 242.

91. 'Soğuk Savaş Kuşatmasında Türkiye, Batı Ve Orta Doğu 1945–1958', 242.

92. 'Soğuk Savaş Kuşatmasında Türkiye, Batı Ve Orta Doğu 1945–1958', 246.

93. 'Soğuk Savaş Kuşatmasında Türkiye, Batı Ve Orta Doğu 1945–1958', 57.

94. Ekavi Athanassopoulou, *Turkey: Anglo-American Security Interests, 1945–1952: The First Enlargement of NATO* (London: Frank Cass, 1999), 76.

95. *Turkey: Anglo-American Security Interests, 1945–1952: The First Enlargement of NATO*, 76.

96. *Turkey: Anglo-American Security Interests, 1945–1952: The First Enlargement of NATO*, 51.

97. Certeau, *The Writing of History*.

Chapter 3

The 'Past' as Experienced

The way Eurocentrism manifests itself in and through historiographical debates in the 'centre' and the 'periphery' was the focus of Chapter 2. This chapter will focus on the manifestations of Eurocentrism in and through the 'past' as experienced.[1] The previous chapters discussed the issues related to conceptualizations of history and underlined the 'past' as it cannot be recovered. This chapter then is not concerned with finding a 'past'. The following 'stories' and 'events' are not organized in a linear and chronological manner but rather in the ways in which Eurocentrism manifested itself. The stories have thus been divided under three main headings. The first section, 'Narrating the International', traces the ways in which the 'international' was discussed at the end of the Second World War. The second section, 'The Cold War', discusses the ways in which Turkey was situated within the narrative of the Cold War. The third section, 'Foreign Agents and Western Democracies', discusses how the term 'Western democracies' was used in discussions with respect to the threat of communism, infiltration of foreign agents and the necessity to establish national unity.

The manifestations of Eurocentrism discussed in this chapter are related mainly to issues of representation. That said, the manifestations need to be taken as being interlinked, and as such, the historical and epistemic variants also come into the story. Gayatri Spivak argues that archives should not be approached as 'facts' but rather 'read'. Thus, through her reading she discusses the ways in which 'soldiers and administrators of the East India Company were constructing the objects of representation that becomes the reality of India'.[2] The chapter then does not focus on 'reading' a story of Turkey's accession to nationhood and to what extent and under what conditions it was able to come to its own. Rather, the chapter focuses on different manifestations of Eurocentrism and the different hierarchies that were reproduced within discussions of the international. The discussions within the period, as can be observed through debates in newspapers, declarations of government officials and parliamentary meetings, worked to reproduce hierarchies between the 'West' and 'Turkey' whereby the West is not only the central subject of history but also the embodiment of democracy and modernization. As such, 'world politics is taken to be happening exclusively in Europe' and discussions of Turkey are 'derivative of European developments' and focus on 'diffusion of European ideas and institutions'.[3]

NARRATING THE INTERNATIONAL

This section will focus on how the 'international system', the Second World War and the United States and Soviet Union were written about at the end of the Second World War. The main focus will be on how Europe and the West are taken as the central subjects of history. In 1947, a *New York Times* correspondent made the following observation with respect to the foreign policy of the United States: 'The Prime Minister expressed his contentment of America leaving its isolationist policies and argued that American involvement will not only help the world but also the United States herself'.[4] More detailed discussions were made in newspapers. Here is an example:

> Ever since gaining its independence 169 years ago United States has served to save the independence of humanity twice. In the first world war American army came to the help of Europe that had lost its strength and hope. ... It has again been this nation that brought in its technical knowledge and military strength and increased the Allies chance of a victory.[5]

This narrative was taken further by Falih Rıfkı Atay, a famous writer, journalist and member of Parliament, who argued, 'American foreign policy has left its isolationist policy and changed its direction after participating in two world wars in 25 years without any calculations or territorial designs. It is no doubt that if this direction had been adopted at the end of the First World War the Second World War would not have happened'.[6] This view is in line with the 'orthodox realist' explanation of the US foreign policy, which argued that

> in 1917–1918, the United States, morally and psychologically unequipped to do so, came into the War at the eleventh hour to restore the balance of power, while pretending that it was doing something altogether different and nobler. The result was that the lesson was not learned the first time, that it had to be repeated in 1941, and that it would finally be learned only in 1947, when at last the United States, now grim and realistic, would abandon its isolationist policy and all its outworn traditions in order to meet the challenges of Stalinist Russia.[7]

In an article written in 1948, Nihat Erim, a member of Parliament from the Republican People's Party, provided an overview of the international system by stating that

> on the one hand Iranian government forces have received orders to enter Azerbaijan lands and on the other hand the change in attitude Molotov displayed in New York. … The tense atmosphere that has existed since the war ended has reached its limit. Especially in recent weeks it has reached a new level when Molotov asked about the number of Allied soldiers in Allied states. The implication of this question was; what is the purpose of these forces. This question was not left unanswered. England and the United States stated that we should not only state how many forces are on the ground but how many forces a state has mobilized. The implication was that the reason behind allied forces in Europe is the large army the Soviet Union has at home.[8]

The interpretation of the Second World War, the international system and Soviet foreign policy aims in this article is in accordance with the traditional US Cold War interpretations that questioned appeasement as a viable policy option, that regarded the Soviet Union as an expansionist power that could not be reasoned with and that concluded that this expansion had to be met with resolution.

The Russian threat is presented as a threat not only to Turkey but also to the region and the international system situating Turkey at its centre.[9] The argument is based on Turkey's credentials as a 'peace-loving nation' that wants to solve issues through international means. Here are the prime minister's words:

> We desire sincere and friendly relations with all our neighbors including our great neighbor Soviet Russia. But the realization of this does not depend solely on our desire. … In view of the overall security, not only of Turkey but also of the Mediterranean region to which Turkey belongs we deem it essential that a Mediterranean defense system should be set up and linked to the general security system provided for under the Atlantic pact.[10]

Internationalizing the problem also meant internationalizing the solution, clearly situating Turkey within the Western Alliance. In its foreign policy declarations, references are made to the United Nations and its principles and how Turkey is an intrinsic part of it by stating that 'our government who has abided by the principles of the United Nations will continue to work for the establishment of peace and security'.[11]

Prime Minister Şükrü Saraçoğlu stated in a speech that the 'aim is to establish deep and genuine friendship bonds, we hope that in order to achieve positive results these efforts are reciprocated. We do not want anything from anyone and we have nothing to give'.[12] This line of argumentation aimed to establish Turkey's role in the new international system as an ally of the 'peace-loving' nations. The United Nations and its principles were established as the basis of the new international system, and Turkey's actions were seen as attempts to follow these principles. Furthermore, the relations with the Soviet Union were included within the general structure of the United Nations: 'The principles established with the UN are more than enough to satisfy the worries Soviet Union has with respect to the defense of the Straits'.[13] According to this perspective, 'it is the duty of every state including Russia to improve inter-state relations in order to establish world peace'.[14]

As such, Soviet actions were framed as being not only a threat to Turkey's sovereignty but also a threat to the new international system being set up by the United States within which Turkey situated itself. The Soviet demands were narrated into the general Soviet actions as proof that they threatened the peace and stability of the international system. In an article criticizing Soviet actions, Nihat Erim stated: 'Soviets have demonstrated lack of trust in the UN system with the administration styles it created in Finland, Lithuania, Estonia, Poland, Romania, Bulgaria and in Iran, and in their policy of intimidation and attrition'.[15] Thus, the Soviet note to Turkey became part of Soviet Union's pattern of challenging the UN system being set up by the United States. It was embedded into the narrative of an expanding Soviet Union that threatened and infiltrated governments with which it shared a border. Furthermore, it was argued that, 'it is only Turkey that has stood against all the pressures'.[16] As such, Turkey was situated on the side of the United States resisting Soviet pressures and upholding the principles of the United Nations. According to this narrative, Soviet Union was threatening the territorial integrity of Turkey and by not giving into its demands Turkey was aiding the international efforts against aggression. Hence, Nihat Erim stated in an article that, 'in no era was the Turkish straits a private matter between Russia and the Turkish nation'.[17] The Soviet note was narrated as being a threat to Turkey and international peace and a possible cause for a Third World War. As such, reacting and criticizing Turkey's policies in this sphere were considered as endangering the national security of the state.

This section focused on how the international was written. Within these renditions, the United States is the central subject of the international system. Furthermore, it is the system that is set up through the United Nations, which is considered as the basis for the international system. As such, Europe and the West remain the main subjects of history.

'THE COLD WAR'

This section will focus on the way Turkey was situated within the Cold War. Turkey's stance during the Second World War was one of the main discussion points, and the underlying theme was that Turkey had always sided with the West. The Soviet notes towards Turkey were one of the main discussion points.[18] As Nihat Erim argued, 'A base means surrendering our sovereign rights. In order to suffer such a punishment one (a state) needs to be a defeated nation. That is why, the day the Russians gave the note the newspapers started publications attempting to make Turkey look guilty in the Second World War'.[19] According to Saraçoğlu, 'Turkey sided with the allies at the first sign of a war' and 'as soon as the war started it mobilized a million soldiers and prepared itself for any possibilities. Germans must have understood the high cost of doing things the hard way. ... We stood with guns until the end of the war, sure of the opinion that we had a role in the war fought in the name of humanity'.[20] The reframing was primarily a reaction to Soviet attacks about Turkey's role in the Second World War but also part of a general reframing of Turkey's place in the international system. The reframing of the narrative focused upon Turkey aligning itself with the 'West' from the start of the war.

This line of argumentation intensified with respect to the Marshall Plan when Turkish officials underlined Turkey's importance and the necessity for further aid in order to keep Turkey as a bulwark against communism. Newspapers published articles asking the government to be more proactive in obtaining American aid, underlining the importance of joining the Atlantic Pact and attempted to underline Turkey's importance in the Cold War. Turkish argument was based on the assumption that Turkey deserved more aid because of its pivotal role in the Cold War and because of its alliance with the West. Sedat Simavi, a journalist and founder of the *Hürriyet* newspaper, stated in an article, 'We have to explain to the Americans that we have a strong army. We are trustworthy people. We do not have communism. As such we deserve the most aid'.[21] Furthermore, he argued, 'Europe has one hope today: the Turkish army'.[22] Turkey's strategic importance in the Cold War divisions was constantly underlined by the press and the government and used as one of the main arguments for more aid.

The main premise of the arguments was Turkey's strategic importance in the Cold War geopolitics.[23] Prime Minister Adnan Menderes argued in an interview, 'In view of the over-all security, not only of Turkey but also of the Mediterranean region to which Turkey belongs, we deem it essential that a Mediterranean defense system should be set up and linked to the general security system provided for under the Atlantic pact'.[24] Turkish foreign policy aims stressed alliances mainly because belonging to one would underline Turkey's acceptance into the Western bloc. As Menderes stated: 'I have stressed the importance we attach to our alliance with Great Britain. ... I believe that it is to the vital interests of both parties that we should strive to further reinforce, in the practical field this alliance which has assumed a national character in Turkey and which has become one of the pillars of our foreign policy'.[25] It is important to note that Menderes defines the alliance with Great Britain as having 'assumed a national character'. Furthermore, he stated: 'Turkey's acceptance into the Atlantic Pact with equal rights has been received with pleasure. This event is an important step in achieving the common security aimed by the Democratic world'.[26] This statement underlines how Turkey was being situated within the international and how the Western Alliance was seen as constituting the 'democratic world'.

The main foreign policy debate centred around the Atlantic Pact and the necessity for accepting Turkey into the pact. In an article in 1950, Necmettin Sadak, foreign minister between 16 January 1947 and 22 May 1950, emphasized that

> whether Turkey enters the Atlantic Pact or not is not only about Turkey's security but also of Europe's. The issue is not Turkey being accepted to this and that pact. Events have shown how inadequate the Atlantic pact is. … Under these circumstances not taking advantage of Turkey's status and strength within the European security system is as much an oversight as leaving Turkey's security out of any contractual obligations.[27]

In an article, Hikmet Bayur, historian and member of Parliament until 1946 from the RPP, the party from which he later resigned, outlined the problems in the international system and the opportunities it presented Turkey:

> The reality of the situation is that Russia is not a direct threat to America. United States has to protect certain states that can constitute support for it so that it is not left facing a Russia that took over a great part of the old world. The Soviets after swallowing most Eastern and Central European states in 1945, have set out to swallow Asia by using local communists … they have swallowed China, now they are swallowing Korea. In this endeavor, Russia at times takes advantage of the nationalistic and anti-imperialist feelings of Asians. For example in Indo-China, nationalists and communists have united in fighting against the French. But if America was not protecting them Russia would have already taken India and Indo-China behind the Iron Curtain and it still might.[28]

Because of these reasons, he argues, neither Asia nor Europe is showing the United States the necessary understanding, and this situation 'provides Turkey an opportunity to play the role of a great power'.[29] These perspectives were based on underlying the strategic importance of Turkey to Cold War dynamics in general and European security system specifically.

This section has discussed the ways in which Turkey was written into the Cold War dynamics. This was done primarily through underlining its geopolitical importance for the Western alliance.[30] In these 'writings', the West and Europe are taken as the primary reference points of events in the international system.[31] The discussions not only demonstrate the manner in which hierarchies between the West and Turkey are reproduced but also how the West remains the central actor in all narratives of the events.

FOREIGN AGENTS AND WESTERN DEMOCRACIES

This section will focus on the way in which the dangers of Soviet Union, communism and foreign agents were framed with respect to taking the West and Europe as the main comparison points. Soviet Union was, as discussed, seen as a threat in the international arena as well as internally through the 'foreign' agents attempting to spread communism. This narrative was countered through arguing for the necessity for stricter internal monitoring in order to preserve national unity.

The debates surrounding the extension of the martial law demonstrated how domestic politics and foreign policy concerns became more interlinked. Furthermore, the debates reveal the manner in which the international system, the Cold War and Turkey's role in it were defined. In a speech explaining domestic and foreign policy, Prime Minister Recep Peker stated: 'When the existence of states are in consideration the main issue is strategy. The area where Martial Law is being imposed is the Marmara area where the Bosphorus is. This is the area that will be first thought of if Turkey is going to be attacked. As a consequence, it is the most important area in establishing Turkey's security'.[32] Furthermore, in describing the present state of the international system, he stated:

> Even though the war between the Allies and Axis powers is over, the guns and bombs of the Second World War have been replaced by an insidious silence. Turkey needs to be alert because in the present danger will not be as obvious as an invasion. Land has been demanded of Turkey. A foreign base has been demanded under the guise of common defense in the Bhosphorus. We live in a period where there has not been a withdrawal of these demands.[33]

As such, the threat Turkey was facing was identified. It was under danger of an external attack and had to be prepared for it by continuing martial law. These discussions framed Turkey's national security with Cold War terms. Thus, it was stated in the parliamentary meetings discussing the law that 'when the great American nation states that peace has not yet been established, that peace is in danger, and one of those areas under the most danger is our borders, some are still indecisive and still don't comprehend the reasons for martial law'.[34] Hence, the reframing was based on the United States's definition of threat and Turkey was positioned within that definition. As stated in the report: 'There is no peace in the world and international trust has not been established. President Truman has pointed out the dark and dangerous situation the world is in his speech to the Congress'.[35] Thus, the danger defined by Truman was adopted to be the primary concern of the Turkish state. Furthermore, it was stated: 'The pain and suffering continued as could be seen in the continuing chaos in Greece. Which nation does not take precautions when her neighbor's house is burning down? Our first precaution is martial law. Martial Law creates order'.[36]

A recurrent theme was the problems being faced in Western European countries. Examples from Greece were given to demonstrate that occupation did not have to happen for communism to be threatening. It was argued, 'Greece is not under occupation. They do not have Serb or Bulgarian gangs in their mountains. All these are because of their own children who are left without any love for their nation once under the influence and service of foreigners'.[37] Such a narrative achieves the vilification of an 'other' sinister enough to corrupt Turkish citizens. Furthermore, it reifies the narrative of national unity since national unity though threatened is still intact for events are not ascribed directly to Turkish citizens but 'foreign agents' and once those foreign agents are dealt with national unity can continue. Internal provocation became the rationale for continuing a certain style of democracy, continuing martial law, closing down parties and limiting general freedoms. As argued:

> The propaganda against the Turkish state that started outside have in no time turned to internal attacks on the regime and state authority. We are for freedom. If communism was not a system that specifically targeted the elimination of freedom we could have allowed it to be discussed. But communism will destroy the freedoms it champions the first chance it gets. Communism is a new form of imperialism. Communism in Turkey is about the survival of the Turkish state.[38]

Furthermore, the turbulence in Greece is given as a reason to be careful since the threat can expand. Moreover, examples from Italy and Belgium were given in newspapers about the dangers posed by communism. Yeni Sabah argued:

> It is clear that communists are creating frenzy in Italy, government searches in communist headquarters found guns, ammunitions and bombs. The communists themselves admitted that they were going to side with the Soviets and create anarchy. Shouldn't necessary precautions be taken against the armament of the fifth column? In the case of an outside attack the army will be busy fighting the enemy. Should it also be expected to deal with domestic sabotage and rebellion?[39]

By giving examples of the dilemmas faced by established democracies in Europe, the article argues: 'We need to learn lessons from these foreign examples as we are just entering the democratic stage'.[40] The implication of these arguments was that Europe with all the established rules and procedures was ill-equipped to deal with the threat of communist infiltration which could not only be solved by large armies. How could Turkey deal with these threats when it had such fragile institutions?

The aim of this section has been to underline how the discussions with respect to how to maintain order against the communist and Soviet threat focused on comparisons with Western democracies. The underlying theme of this section was the reproduction of the hierarchies between the West and Turkey and situating democracy within the West.

CONCLUSION

The snippets of the story presented so far do not mean that there were not challenges to the alliance with the West. For example, in a letter to the prime minister in 1951, Zekeriya Sertel, a journalist, argued:

I don't think Turkey's entrance to the Atlantic Pact is possible nor is it desirable. Considering the fragile nature of Turkey's geopolitical position, the only policy that will ensure its safety is neutrality. Unfortunately since all ideas in the country are under certain influences being directed towards a certain direction and since any differing opinion are being branded as traitors those who want to establish friendly relations with the Soviets as Atatürk suggested are being silenced and neutrality policy is no longer discussed nor is it possible to be defended. Since the times of İsmet İnönü Turkey has always been careful to align its policies with the United States and has never considered the possibility of other policies. Even today American and Western guarantees are pursued, when in reality the most serious, safe and healthy policy is that of neutrality. It can be argued that there can no longer be a small neutral country and Turkey once forced to choose a side had to side with the democracies.[41]

The criticism of the government with regard to establishing friendly relations with the Soviet Union and not 'taking sides' was seen as the basis for an independent Turkish foreign policy. As stated by Zekeriya Sertel: 'History has made us neighbors with the Soviets. ... Soviet Union is no longer Tsarist Russia. It would be stupid to ignore this historical change. Soviets could have no aims towards Turkey other than friendship. For a Turkey that has experienced the pains of imperialism the right path is friendship with the Soviets'.[42] The argument was not to forsake one side for the other but to establish friendly relations with all without becoming entangled in great power politics. Sertel further stated: 'We said that let's expand the alliance with Britain and make one with the United States and Russia. Russia's position as a strong state and

as our northern neighbor will not change. History has proven that it is in our
interest to live in peace with our neighbor. We want friendship with all states
for the sake of Turkey'.[43] The criticisms of the government also underlined
dangers of imperialism and that the foreign aid being received would be det-
rimental to Turkey's independence. In that vein, Sabahattin Ali, a novelist,
poet and journalist, argued:

> Foreign investment will return to our country. While giving this news newspa-
> pers are rejoicing. Official authorities are aiding the entry of foreign money into
> the nation.
>
> Once this investment comes, motorways will run, the cities will be filled with
> airplanes, the nation will be filled with goods.
>
> Then what was the purpose of the struggle to eradicate foreign investment in
> the last forty years.
>
> Now I remember. I was just a five or six year old child. Mobilization had
> begun. The adventurist government of the time tried to sugar coat this bloody
> adventure by shouting;
>
> 'Capitulations are removed'
>
> During the four years mobilization and three year Independence War we were
> told to be fighting in order to rid ourselves of the semi-colonization foreign
> investment had caused.
>
> If we were going to invite them with open arms, why did we throw them out
> with celebrations?[44]

Thus, there was resistance to opening Turkey to foreign and Western influences. These efforts for alternative perspectives and narratives on 'Turkey's'
position in the international system though 'resisting' the main narrative also
still work within pre-established conceptualizations of the international and
in and through an idea of 'Turkey' and 'national unity'.

The chapter has focused on the manifestations of Eurocentrism within the
'past' as experienced, focusing on the ways in which the West was seen as
the centre of history and democracy. Just as the examples presented here do
not mean to imply the non-existence of alternative reframings, nor do they
suggest that there were not contextual reasons for the positions adopted.[45]
The aim of the chapter has been to demonstrate the way in which manifestations of Eurocentrism permeate all levels of inquiry whether it be the historiographical debates, as discussed in Chapter 2, or the 'past' as experienced,
as discussed in this chapter. The first section, 'Narrating the International',
traced the ways in which the 'international' was discussed at the end of the
Second World War. The second section, 'The Cold War', discussed the ways
in which 'Turkey' was situated within the narrative of the Cold War and the
Western alliance. The third section, 'Foreign Agents and Western Democracies', discussed how the term 'Western democracies' was used in discussions

with respect to the threat of communism and infiltration of foreign agents and the necessity to establish national unity. The aim of this chapter had been to underline the different manifestations of Eurocentrism, whether culturalist, historical and epistemic, in the workings of history, historiography and the 'past' as experienced. The main points underlined were how the hierarchies between the West and Turkey were reproduced in discussions about the international system, the importance and centrality of the United States, the threat of communism and the Soviet Union.

The aim of Section II, 'Manifestations of Eurocentrism', will be to trace the different ways in which Eurocentrism manifests itself in and through disciplines and geopolitical contexts. It has been argued that the story of Eurocentrism has to take into account not only the ways in which it manifests in one disciplinary formation such as International Relations but also how these manifestations are connected and intertwined. As such, tracing the manifestations of Eurocentrism in and through disciplinary formations and geopolitical contexts underscores the need for connected histories, in order to tackle the issue of Eurocentrism. Furthermore, as the next section, 'Criticisms of Eurocentrism', will underline, the criticisms of Eurocentrism and the connections in and between disciplinary formations and geopolitical knowledges are also important.

NOTES

1. The archives that were consulted were the T. C. Başbakanlık Devlet Arşivleri and Atatürk IBB Kitapliği.

2. Gayatri Chakravorty Spivak, 'The Rani of Sirmur: An Essay in Reading the Archives', *History and Theory* 24, no. 3 (1985): 247–272.

3. Barkawi and Laffey, 'The Postcolonial Moment in Security Studies', 335.

4. 'New York Times Correspondent on Turkey', in *Cumhuriyet Arşivi, Başbakanlık Devlet Arşivleri* (File: A6, Code: 30..1.0.0, Place:12.70.5.17 April 1947).

5. Esat Tekeli, 'America's Independence Day', in *Ulus* (Atatürk IBB Kitapliği, Cilt 4, Sayı 8961–91446 July 1945).

6. Falih Rifkı Atay, 'Decisiveness in Foreign Policy', in *Ulus* (Atatürk IBB Kitapliği, Cilt 4, Sayı 8961–91448 October 1946).

7. Halle, *The Cold War as History*, 26.

8. 'Nihat Erim, in the Face of a Complicated Picture, Ulus Newspaper, 1 December 1948', in *Cumhuriyet Arşivi, Başbakanlık Devlet Arşivleri* (File: A6, Code: 0.30.01, Place: 11.68.2, 1 December 1948).

9. On how the Soviet 'threat' was constructed, see Kıvanç Coş and Pınar Bilgin, 'Stalin's Demands: Constructions of the "Soviet Other" in Turkey's Foreign Policy, 1919–1945', *Foreign Policy Analysis* 6, no. 1 (2010): 43–60.

10. 'Questions Submitted to H.E. M. Adnan Menderes, Prima Minister of Turkey, by Mr. Ralph Izzard, Special Correspondent to the Daily Mail, London, 5 June

1950', in *Cumhuriyet Arşivi, Başbakanlık Devlet Arşivleri* (File: E4, Code: 30..1.0.0, Place:60.372..2.).

11. 'Nihat Erim, "in the Face of a Complicated Nature", Ulus, 1 December 1948', in *Cumhuriyet Arşivi, Başbakanlık Devlet Arşivleri* (File: A6, Code: 30..1.0.0, Place: 11.68.6.).

12. 'Meeting with Journalists, Sukru Saracoglu', in *Cumhuriyet Arsivi, Cumhuriyet Arşivi, Başbakanlık Devlet Arşivleri* (File: 16, Code: 30..1.0.0, Place: 11.64.65 September 1945).

13. 'M. Philips Price, Turkish Pm's Views on the Straits Issue, Manchester Guardian, 30.11.1946', in *Cumhuriyet Arşivi, Başbakanlık Devlet Arşivleri* (File: A6, Code: 0.30.01, Place: 11.67.3.).

14. 'M. Philips Price, Turkish Pm's Views on the Straits Issue, Manchester Guardian, 30.11.1946'.

15. Nihat Erim, 'The Only Missing Link, Ulus, 18 August 1946' (Atatürk IBB Kitapliği, Cilt 4, Sayı 8961–9144).

16. 'The Only Missing Link, Ulus, 18 August 1946'.

17. 'Reaction to the Soviet Note, Ulus, 24 August 1946' (Atatürk IBB Kitapliği, Cilt 4, Sayı 8961–9144).

18. Coş and Bilgin, 'Stalin's Demands: Constructions of the "Soviet Other" in Turkey's Foreign Policy, 1919–1945'.

19. Nihat Erim, 'With Respect to Russian Demands, Ulus, 15 August 1946' (Atatürk IBB Kitapliği, Cilt 4, Sayı 8961–9144).

20. 'Prime Minister's Speech, 6.4.1946', in *Cumhuriyet Arşivi, Başbakanlık Devlet Arşivleri* (File:A6, Code: 0.30.01, Place: 11.65.2.).

21. Sedat Simavi, 'American Aid, Hurriyet, 14 January 1951', in *Cumhuriyet Arşivi, Başbakanlık Devlet Arşivleri* (File: 1. BURO, Code:490..1.0.0, Place:204.811.3.).

22. 'American Aid, Hurriyet, 14 January 1951'.

23. Pınar Bilgin, 'Only Strong States Can Survive in Turkey's Geography: The Uses of "Geopolitical Truths" in Turkey', *Political Geography* 26, no. 7 (2007): 740–756; 'Turkey's "Geopolitics Dogma"'.

24. 'Questions Submitted to H.E. M. Adnan Menderes, Prima Minister of Turkey, by Mr. Ralph Izzard, Special Correspondent to the Daily Mail, London, 5 June 1950'.

25. 'Questions Submitted to H.E. M. Adnan Menderes, Prima Minister of Turkey, by Mr. Ralph Izzard, Special Correspondent to the Daily Mail, London, 5 June 1950'.

26. 'Decleration by Pm Adnan Menderes, 21.2.1951', in *Cumhuriyet Arşivi, Başbakanlık Devlet Arşivleri* (File A6, Code: 0.30.01, Place: 13.76.7.).

27. Necmeddin Sadak, 'Atlantic Pact and Turkey, Aksam, 15.08.1950', in *Cumhuriyet Arşivi, Başbakanlık Devlet Arşivleri* (File: 408, Code: 1.204, Place: 809.1.).

28. Hikmet Bayur, 'America, Asia, Europe and Us, Kudret, 21.08.1950', in *Cumhuriyet Arşivi, Başbakanlık Devlet Arşivleri* (File: 408, Code: 1.204, Place: 809.1.).

29. 'America, Asia, Europe and Us, Kudret, 21.08.1950'.

30. Eylem Yılmaz and Pınar Bilgin, 'Constructing Turkey's "Western" Identity During the Cold War: Discourses of the Intellectuals of Statecraft', *International Journal* 61, no. 1 (2005): 39–59.

31. It should be noted that this is not to argue that these attitudes were not rooted in insecurities from the international system. For further information, see, Bilgin, 'Securing Turkey through Western-Oriented Foreign Policy'.

32. 'Parliament Meeting, 28.5.1947', in *Cumhuriyet Arşivi, Başbakanlık Devlet Arşivleri* (File: A6, Code: 30.01, Place: 12.71.3.).

33. 'Parliament Meeting, 28.5.1947'.

34. 'Parliament Meeting, 28.5.1947'.

35. 'Parliament Meeting, 28.5.1947'.

36. 'Parliament Meeting, 28.5.1947'.

37. 'An Important Example, Ulus, 7 September 1946' (Atatürk Kitapliği, Cilt 4, Sayı 8961–9144).

38. 'You Can Not Threaten the Existence of the Turkish Nation, Ulus, 18 December 1946' (Atatürk Kitapliği, Cilt 4, Sayı 8961–9144).

39. 'Yeni Sabah, Newspaper Clippings, 8 August 1950'.

40. 'Yeni Sabah, Newspaper Clippings, 8 August 1950'.

41. 'Zekeriya Sertel's Letter, 24 April 1951', *Cumhuriyet Arşivi, Başbakanlık Devlet Arşivleri* (File: B2, Code: 30..1.0.0, Place: 41.243..9.).

42. Zekeriya Sertel, *Hatirladıklarım* (Istanbul: Remzi Kitabevi, 1977).

43. *Hatirladıklarım*.

44. Foreign Investment, Sabahattin Ali, Markopaşa, 2 Aralık 1946 (Markopaşa Yazıları ve Ötekiler, 124–125).

45. Yilmaz and Bilgin, 'Constructing Turkey's "Western" Identity During the Cold War: Discourses of the Intellectuals of Statecraft'; Bilgin, *The International in Security, Security in the International*.

Section II

CRITICISMS OF EUROCENTRISM

Section I discussed the different manifestations of Eurocentrism in and through disciplines focusing on the relationship between history and international relations. The chapters specifically focused on the different levels in which these conversations happened and continue to happen. Section II aims to discuss the criticisms of Eurocentrism in and through disciplines and geopolitical knowledges. The focus of the section will be on the theoretical approaches that deal with the problematique of Eurocentrism and knowledge production. The aim is to underline the connections and conversations that exist in and through different theoretical strategies. It also points to the different conversations that continue in and between disciplines, as the theoretical strategies being discussed are not rooted in one 'discipline' and move between different disciplines.

Chapter 4, 'Coloniality, Postcoloniality, Decoloniality', focuses on the different conversations that occurred in and between the theoretical strategies developed to problematize Eurocentrism. The tracing of the development of theoretical strategies aiming to criticize Eurocentrism aims to demonstrate an array of connections and conversations in and through disciplinary formations and geopolitical knowledges underlying the different manifestations of criticisms of Eurocentrism. The chapter aims to underline how the 'academic disciplines' have worked to construct a canon for both postcolonial studies and decolonial thought. There are presences and absences in these narratives that not only disrupt the linearity of the story but also make one question the situatedness of these theoretical discourses in 'academic fields'.

Chapter 5, 'Constructing the Non-Western', focuses on the way in which the theoretical strategies that problematize Eurocentrism have entered into conversation with the discipline of International Relations. The chapter aims to underline the way in which criticisms of Eurocentrism manifested itself in a certain way within International Relations because of the disciplinary formations of the field and the privileged concerns it had.

Chapter 4

Coloniality, Decoloniality, Postcoloniality

This chapter focuses on the conversations that occurred in and between the theoretical strategies developed to problematize Eurocentrism. The tracing of the development of theoretical strategies aiming to criticize Eurocentrism demonstrates an array of connections and conversations in and through disciplinary formations and geopolitical knowledges underlying the different manifestations of criticisms of Eurocentrism. The chapter will proceed in three parts. The first part will discuss the main debates in and around postcolonial theory and the different conversations within that theoretical space that exists in and between disciplines and geopolitical knowledges. The second part will trace the different ways in which postcolonial theory and the postcolonial condition were engaged within and through disciplines and within different geopolitical knowledges. The third part will discuss the main debates within decolonial thought. The aim of the chapter is to discuss the manifestations of the criticisms of Eurocentrism in and through disciplinary formations and geopolitical knowledges.

'LOCATING' POSTCOLONIAL THEORY

How to locate postcolonial theory? This is a loaded question in more ways than one, and postcolonial theory has been the source of many debates.[1] One of the persistent debates has been the naming of the 'field of study'. What does the 'post' in the postcolonial designate? Is it a temporal or a historical periodization? As Neil Lazarus points out, the term 'postcolonialism' existed and was used before the existence of the field of study, though in a much different manner and mainly 'as a periodizing term, an historical and not an ideological concept', and, as such, 'it bespoke no political desire or aspiration,

looked forward to no particular social or political order'.[2] The implications
of a temporal and historical designation in the word 'post'[3] signal issues with
respect to the exact beginning of the term 'postcolonial' and the different
relationships between different 'beginnings'. As such, the term 'downplays
multiplicities of location and temporality, as well as the possible discursive
and political linkages between "postcolonial" theories and contemporary
anti-colonial, or anti neo-colonial struggles and discourses'.[4] Furthermore,
the prefix 'post' works to situate postcolonialism 'on the border between old
and new, end and beginning' signalling 'the end of a world era, but within
the same trope of linear progress that animated that era'.[5] These concerns,
which stem from the 'naming' of the 'field of study', signal deeper issues that
continue to be important debating points within postcolonial studies, whether
with respect to the different and diverse experiences of colonialism and postcolonialism or with respect to the ways in which postcolonial analysis can at
times become complicit in reproducing the very dynamics it criticizes and
how to overcome that dynamic.

When do we then begin the story of postcolonial studies? Robert Young
argues that 'it was Said's critique in Orientalism (1978) of the cultural politics
of academic knowledge' that 'effectively founded postcolonial studies as an
academic discipline'.[6] Orientalism was approached as 'the corporate institu-
tion for dealing with the Orient – dealing with it by making statements about
it, authorizing views of it, describing it, by teaching it, settling it, ruling over
it' and was thus 'a Western style for dominating, restructuring, and having
authority over the Orient'.[7] Young states that 'postcolonial studies have actually defined itself as an academic discipline through the range of objections,
reworkings and counter-arguments that have been marshalled in such great
variety against Said's work'.[8] In that sense, criticisms towards Said's work
also reveal the main debating points that have been present in postcolonial
studies since the 1980s. Furthermore, as *Orientalism* sets the main debating
point through underlying the relationship between academic knowledge and
power, the task becomes not only to discuss and identify different manifestations of this relationship but also to ponder the question about how to produce knowledge that does not continue the same system of dominating and
restructuring. Said himself ponders this question in 'Orientalism Considered'
and asks 'how knowledge that is non-dominative and non-coercive can be
produced in a setting that is deeply inscribed with the politics, the considerations, the positions, and the strategies of power'.[9] The question remains to
this day and looms into any discussion on 'postcolonialism' with or without
the hyphen.

Edward Said's influence is undoubtedly present in what is generally termed
'postcolonial studies', and the debates and disagreements that exist within
the 'field' continue to be formulated in and through Edward Said's work.

This should not be taken to mean that Edward Said was the 'first' to make these arguments or that discussions of Orientalism did not exist before.[10] Edward Said's influence is tied to two main dynamics: first, to the general academic environment and the 'discursive shift in literary studies, history and anthropology animated by poststructuralism, Western feminism, and neo-Marxism'[11]; and secondly, to the interdisciplinary nature of his work and how it has become 'a model for navigating between literature, history, philosophy, and anthropology'.[12] The influence of Orientalism can also be observed through the debate it generated and the manner in which the drawbacks in his arguments were taken up to be furthered. One of the main drawbacks of *Orientalism*, as Aijaz Ahmad so succinctly puts it, has been that it 'examines the history of Western textualities about the non-West quite in isolation from how these textualities might have been received, accepted, modified, challenged, overthrown and reproduced by the intelligentsia of the colonized countries' and 'not as an undifferentiated mass but as situated social agents impelled by our own conflicts, contradictions, distinct social and political locations, of class, gender, region, religious affiliation'.[13] The main sub-strands developed signal to different debates and discussions regarding postcolonial studies, colonial discourse analysis and subaltern studies. The colonial discourse analysis in and through the work of Jacques Derrida, Michel Foucault and Jacques Lacan focused on the representation of colonial subjects. Homi Bhabha and Gayatri Spivak are generally seen as the main representatives of this body of work, though Spivak is also associated with the Subaltern Studies Group, underlying the need not to make categorical distinctions.

Homi Bhabha aims to further the picture presented by Edward Said. He argues that the representation of the colonized that creates the categories and constructs the colonized cannot be seen as fixed and underlines that these constructions are never complete because 'colonial discourse produces the colonised as a social reality which is at once an "other" and yet entirely knowable and visible'.[14] The process thus brings the *colonized* within the categories of Western knowledge to make them knowable on terms determined by the *colonizer*, but these depictions and categorizations also continue to reproduce the distance between the colonizer and the colonized. As such, the constructions of categories always remain ambivalent and always necessitate repetition. Bhabha uses the example of the Indian who being educated in English works as an in-between between the imperial power and the colonized people and, as such, 'the look of surveillance returns as the displacing gaze of the disciplined, where the observer becomes the observed and the "partial" representation rearticulates the who notion of *identity* and alienates it from essence'.[15] Thus, through the notions of ambivalence and mimicry Bhabha is able to bring agency to the discussion of the relationship between the knowledge produced about the colonized.

Gayatri Spivak is harder to pinpoint in terms of genealogy as she is usually situated with both colonial discourse and subaltern studies. Spivak's reading of Jane Eyre and Bertha Mason focuses on the subaltern position of Bertha Mason in the novel. Thus, 'In this fictive England, [Bertha] must play out her role, act out the transformation of her "self" into that fictive Other, set fire to the house and kill herself' in order to enable Jane Eyre to 'become the feminist individualist heroine of British fiction', which is read 'as an allegory of the general epistemic violence of imperialism, the construction of a self-immolating colonial subject for the glorification of the social mission of the colonizer'.[16] This underlines how critiques of patriarchy work to silence the colonial context that made their articulation possible.[17] What the colonial discourse analysis achieves is demonstrate and discuss the different trajectories through which the colonial subject was constituted, negotiated and reproduced in the colonial context.

Subaltern studies was motivated through the need to re-write Indian nationalist and imperial historiography.[18] The Subaltern Studies Group emerged in the 1980s, and its main aim was to criticize the Nationalist and Cambridge School of Indian history. As such, it was an intervention into the subject of Indian history from a postcolonial and subaltern perspective. The starting point for Ranajit Guha was the elitism of the historiography of Indian nationalism. Within the mainstream writings, the history of Indian nationalism was primarily presented as a 'learning experience' that helped the elite lead the people to freedom. These stories of Indian nationalism do not explain 'the contribution made by the people *on their own*, that is, *independently of the elite* to the making and development of nationalism'.[19] Arif Dirlik famously argued that the perspectives of subaltern studies 'represent the application in Indian historiography of trends in historical writing that were quite widespread by the 1970s under the impact of social historians such as E.P. Thompson, Eric Hobsbawm, and a host of others'.[20] The extent to which this argument holds is questioned by Dipesh Chakrabarty, who argues that one of the main breaks of the subaltern studies came with its redefinition of the category of the 'pre-political' and 'political'. Looking at collective action in colonial India worked to extend the category of the 'political' because assigning peasant consciousness to a 'pre-political' category would mean that 'the discourses of kinship, caste, religion, and ethnicity through which they expressed themselves in protest' would only be assigned 'as a "backward" consciousness'.[21] Subaltern studies itself was not a uniform group, and scholars associated with it worked in different trajectories. Furthermore, during the second Subaltern Studies Conference held in Calcutta in January 1986, there was already a division between 'greater concentration on textual analysis and a stress on the relativity of all knowledge' and 'the study of subaltern consciousness and action so as to forward the struggle for a social society'.[22]

In many ways, as Robert Young states, these figures are considered the 'Holy Trinity'[23] of postcolonial studies. In that sense, the story of postcolonial studies has in itself a narrative of 'great debates', similar to that of International Relations, the retelling of which also reproduces the main boundaries of the debate as we focus on the colonial discourse and Subaltern Studies Group. There are in reality many different currents in and between the different categorizations. Furthermore, as Bart-Moore Gilbert states, 'Postcolonial criticism and theory alike comprise a variety of practices, performed within a range of disciplinary fields in a multitude of different institutional locations around the globe', and the issue of the beginning and the main 'proponents' cannot be read through the 'Holy Trinity'.[24] As such, it would need to elaborate on figures such as W. E. B. Du Bois, 'discuss cultural formations as diverse as the Harlem Renaissance of World War One and the 1920s and the *negritude* movement of the 1940s and 1950s' and would also need to visit the writings of C. L. R. James, Frantz Fanon and Aime Cesaire since it was never a 'smooth narrative of "influence and development"'.[25]

ENGAGING THE POSTCOLONIAL

Postcolonial studies in general and subaltern studies in particular were discussed in and through disciplines and geopolitical knowledges. The way in which the 'postcolonial' came to be understood in the Western Academy (though the 'name' Western is utilized, it is dominantly the Anglo-American academic space that is being referred to)[26] was engaged with differently in different postcolonialities as well.

Frederick Cooper discusses the trajectories of the historiographies in African history and the Subaltern Studies Group where he underlines that 'Subaltern Studies emerged in the 1980s, nearly forty years after India's independence' and because of that focused on criticism of established historiographies whether Marxist or nationalist.[27] In contrast, because 'Africa's independence movements are more recent, their histories only beginning to be written' their ' disillusionment with the fruits of independence in the 1970s took the form of an emphasis on the external determinants of economic and social problems, and hence a look towards Latin American dependency theory'.[28] Thus, when, where and how independence happened was a determinant in the priorities accorded to discussions of postcoloniality.[29] This is reminiscent of the issues signalled to with respect to the 'naming' of the 'field of study'. When, where and how the 'postcolonial' is determines the manner in which the criticism and resistance was formulated. Thus, India's experience differed from that of African independence movements and as it also did from that of the Latin American and Middle Eastern ones. As a result, there are different historiographical traditions that can be underlined. For example, K. Onwuka Dike attempted to challenge imperial historiographies and is generally considered as one of the founders of the Ibadan school of history, which aimed to develop an 'African perspective of history'.[30] Dike argues:

> In the years before the Second World War, the study of African history was retarded, and to some extent vitiated, by the assumption of many scholars that lack of written records in some areas of Africa meant also the absence of history. Documentary evidence had become so overwhelmingly important for the European scholar that he tended to equate written documents with history, and to take the absence of documents to mean the absence of events worthy of historical study. As a result in the nineteenth century, when Europe occupied Africa, her scholars did not attempt to understand or to build on the historical traditions in existence there; they sought instead to challenge and to supplant them. The history of European traders, missionaries, explorers, conquerors and rulers constituted, in their view, the sum total of African history.[31]

Walter Rodney, author of *How Europe Underdeveloped Africa*, was part of the Dar es Salaam 'school' and took part in a famous debate with Ali Mazrui in 1970 at Makerere University in Uganda.[32] The Dar es Salaam school was from the beginning attracting

> staff interested in socialism, especially in the Faculty of Arts and Social Sciences. The historian Walter Rodney, from Guyana, was probably the most well known. In political science John Saul and Lionel Cliffe formed a powerful team. ... Their work could be seen in the numbers of papers published by the research bureaux in the early years, and in the establishment of a 'Dar es Salaam view of history', with its slogan of 'putting the African back into African history' popularized by the first professor of history, Terence Ranger, and carried through in the collection of articles *A History of Tanzania* edited by two Tanzanian lecturers in the Department (I. Kimambo and A. Temu) and published in 1969.[33]

This period also included discussions with respect to interdisciplinarity and how 'traditional Western division of social science into economics, political science, sociology, geography, etc., was irrelevant in an underdeveloped country building socialism'.[34] These discussions on 'history' and 'disciplinarity' were not informed by and cannot be classified as part of 'postcolonial theory', but they were thinking and writing about their own postcolonial situation and how to overcome it.

The attempts to make sense of postcoloniality and think through postcolonial thought were also present in Latin America. In the introductory statement to the special issue on 'Postmodernism in Latin America',[35] it is stated that 'liberation theology is itself part of the postmodernist turn in Latin America', though, at the same time, 'liberation theology contests positions and attitudes often associated with postmodernism in the name of a narrative of historical continuity and redemption that it composes out of elements taken from traditional Marxism, Christian eschatalogy, and popular and indigenous cultural memory'.[36] The complex relationship to postmodernity in Latin America is elaborated upon in Anibal Quijano's contribution to the special issue in which he argues that 'it is not only a European-North American discussion or a snobbish, vulgar imposition of a topic foreign to Latin America'.[37] Furthermore, because of the 'reproduction of [Latin American] dependence with respect to European-North American domination', there is a 'permanent note of dualism in our intellectual manner, our sensibility, our imaginary' which cannot be 'simplistically explained by the opposition between the modern and the nonmodern'.[38] Because of this dualism, 'every time there is a crisis in European rationality and, consequently, in the intersubjective relations between the European and the Latin American, the process of the sedimentation of our own identity also enters into crisis, and we once again leave in search of our own identity'.[39] This sense of crisis then also opens up space to rearticulate and renegotiate the identities under crisis and elaborate on ways to rethink and re-evaluate the continuing dualism.

The special issue also contains the founding statement of the Latin American Subaltern Studies Group. The founding statement explains the development of subaltern studies in Latin American studies through phases. The first phase was between 1960 and 1968. The main event in this phase is the Cuban Revolution and the revival of resistance against Eurocentric knowledge. Roberto Fernandez Retamar's reading of Frantz Fanon is given as an example of new ways of writing Latin American history. Furthermore, the appearance of dependency school theorists is also categorized within this phase. The statement notes that these works encountered issues when issues of gender, race and language were brought into the discussion. The second phase was between 1968 and 1979, in which the main event is the collapse of guerrilla fronts, especially that of Che Guevera. Furthermore, this phase is underlined by the coming to the stage of the students. It is in this stage that the dominance of Marxism is destabilized through the introduction of French poststructuralist theory, Gramscian Marxism and Frankfurt School. The third phase is the 1980s, with the main event being identified as the Nicaraguan Revolution and liberation theology. This is the phase when cultural studies enters into Latin American studies.[40] The stated mission is 'to represent subalternity in Latin America, in whatever form it takes wherever it appears – nation, hacienda, work place, home, informal sector, black market – to find the blank space where it speaks as a sociopolitical subject, requires us to explore the margins of the state'.[41]

The review article by Patricia Seed entitled 'Colonial and Postcolonial Discourse'[42] in which she underlines the attraction of poststructuralism ignited a debate, and a special forum was organized in the same journal.[43] In the article, she argues that it is due to 'appropriation and manipulation of its ideas by textual communities outside the West, communities that have found in its attack on traditional humanism and recognition of the plasticity of language powerful resonances with critiques already being developed in their own political and cultural contexts'.[44] In the reply, Walter Mignolo stresses two points: the *locus of enunciation* and *colonial semiosis*. First, he underlines that there is a different quality to Latin American colonial history, meaning that there is a genealogy that is longer and different than the one postcolonial studies operate with. Building on this observation, he asks the question, 'who is writing about what, where and why'. He traces the critique of colonial discourse to Edmundo O'Gorman, who wrote two influential books in the 1950s: *la idea del descrubrimiento de America* and *la invencion de America*, which represents 'the early dismantling of colonial discourse'. O'Gorman is writing not only before the postcolonial studies and colonial discourse analysis but also before post-structuralism. Though, as Miglono points out, he is not writing from a completely different perspective as it was his reading of Heidegger's book *Being and Time* that influenced him. The concept of *colonial semiosis* is brought as a corrective to the text-focused approach of colonial discourse, bringing into focus 'complex system of semiotic interactions embodied in the discursive (oral) and textual (material inscriptions in different writing systems)'.[45]

The engagement with the postcolonial, with or without the hyphen, has incited many debates that are at the same time both more and less than the contours of the postcolonial theoretical space. It is not postcolonial theory as such that is restricting but rather the establishment of canonical works and 'great debates' through which it is made intelligible within academic discourses. Any linearity imposed on the 'postcolonial' is further disrupted with the myriad of intertwined histories it has with both poststructuralist[46] and Marxist thought.[47] Thus, Young argues that 'if so-called poststructuralism is the product of a single historical moment, then that moment is probably not May 1968 but rather the Algerian war of independence'.[48] Moreover, the using of 'poststructuralist' thought in postcolonial thought does not mean a replication but can also be considered as an 'attempt to extend the geographical and historical terrain for the poststructuralist discontent with Western epistemology'.[49]

As such, looking at the myriad of conversations that happened in and through anti-colonial thought a picture is presented whereby the 'origins' and 'journey' of postcolonial thought becomes both more and less than the spaces within which the postcolonial is situated. The next section focuses on the 'emergence' of decolonial thought and discusses in which ways it intervened in the conversations discussed in this section.

DECOLONIALITY

The 1998 meetings at Duke University between South Asian Subaltern Studies Group and Latin American Subaltern Studies Group, after which the Latin American Subaltern Studies Group split, was indicative of the issues being faced in and between the two groups. One of the issues 'was between those who read subalternity as a postmodern critique ... and those who read subalternity as a decolonial critique'.[50] Thus, the Latin Americanist scholars in the United States ended up reproducing 'the epistemic schema of Area Studies' and 'studies about the subaltern rather than studies with and from a subaltern perspective'.[51] The historical ties and the disagreements are elaborated in detail in *Local Histories/Global Designs*, where Walter Mignolo primarily focuses on the divisions between postcoloniality and postmodernism in articulating the differences between the perspectives.[52] In the introduction to *The Darker Side of Modernity*, Walter Mignolo traces his own journey of 'discovering' the concept of coloniality. As he recounts,

> I was in Bogota and found a book just published: *Los conquistados: 1492 y la poblacion indigena de las Americas*, edited by Heraclio Bonilla (1992). The last chapter of that book caught my attention. It was by Anibal Quijano, of whom I had heard, but with whom I was not familiar. ... I devoured the essay, the reading of which was sort of epiphany. ... I concentrated on 'coloniality' which became a central concept in *Local Histories/Global Designs: Coloniality, Subaltern Knowledge and Border Thinking (2000).*[53]

Anibal Quijano argued that 'with the conquest of the societies and the cultures which inhabit what today is called Latin America, began the constitution of a new world order' which resulted in a 'global power covering the whole planet'.[54] Even though colonial domination in its political and explicit case had been defeated, 'the specific colonial structure of power' produced 'specific social discriminations ... codified as "racial", "ethnic", "anthropological" or "national"', which were 'assumed to be "objective", "scientific", "categories"'.[55] This structure continues in the present. As such, coloniality does not refer to 'colonialism' but argues that decolonization in the juridico-political sense did not bring about the eradication of the colonial structure of power. Thus, coloniality refers to 'colonial situations' such as the 'cultural, political, sexual, spiritual, epistemic and economic oppression/exploitation of subordinate racialized/ethnic groups by dominant racialized/ethnic groups with or without the existence of colonial administrations'.[56]

This conceptualization has been developed further within the writings of Walter Mignolo, Nelson Maldonado-Torres and Maria Lugones. Nelson Maldonado-Torres expands upon coloniality of power through the concept

of 'coloniality of being', which focused on the 'lived experience of colonization and its impact on language'.[57] The coloniality of being focuses on 'those
aspects that produce exception from the order of Being' which in order to
'maintain its integrity and inhibit the interruption by what lies beyond Being
produces its contrary', which is not nothing 'but a non-human'.[58] Lugones
introduces gender as being constituted by coloniality and modernity and argues
that 'colonialism did not impose precolonial, European gender arrangements
on the colonized' but rather 'imposed a new gender system that created very
different arrangements for colonized males and females'.[59] She thus compli-
cates Quijano's articulation of coloniality by underlining that 'gender does not
need to organize social arrangements, including social sexual arrangements';
in fact, 'gender arrangements need not be either heterosexual or patriarchal'.[60]

The differences between decoloniality and postcolonialist theories are
mainly related to the different locations from which they emanated and the
different time frames through which coloniality is analysed. The 'difference'
such as it is thus related to the 'colonial difference' and the way 'theories
travel' in and through the colonial difference. With respect to 'travelling
theories' Edward Said argues that 'like people and schools of criticism, ideas
and theories travel – from person to person, from situation to situation, from
one period to another'.[61] Furthermore, he argues that it needs to be specified
what 'kinds of movement are possible' and 'whether by virtue of having
moved from one place and time to another an idea or a theory gains or loses
in strength, and whether a theory in one historical period and national culture becomes altogether different for another period or situation'.[62] Mignolo
builds on the idea of theories travelling and asks the question, 'What happens
when theories travel through the colonial difference?'[63] But a further question is, 'How are they rehearsed when they travel through the colonial difference? Are they just being rehearsed in a new scenario or do they face their
limits in that new scenario?'[64] Furthermore, he underlines that some theories
do not travel because 'the colonial difference makes them invisible to the
mainstream and universal scope of theories that can travel'.[65] It is this consideration of the colonial difference that leads to an underlining of the complex
and varied structures of power relations and the importance of geopolitics of
knowledge. Within this formulation Mignolo suggests, 'critical border thinking' as a 'method that connects pluriversality (different colonial histories
entangled with imperial modernity) into a uni-versal project of delinking
from modern rationality and building other possible worlds'.[66]

CONCLUSION

The role of stories in our imaginations is not only to tell tales of faraway
magical lands but also to bring sequential order to events, to define who we

are, where we belong and where we intend to go. It is within that tradition of storytelling that every story has a beginning, development and end. The aim of the chapter has been to tell a story disconnected and connected at the same time. It is disconnected because the linearity and 'evolution' of categories is not taken as a given, but it is connected because it aims to discuss the relationships that are usually overlooked. The aim has not been to impose linearity but to demonstrate the multiplicity of conversations being had.

Benita Parry, in criticizing colonial discourse studies, argues, rightfully so, that 'the construction of a text disrupting imperialism's authorized version was begun long ago within the political and intellectual cultures of colonial liberation movements, and the counter-discourse developed in this milieu'.[67] Thus, the 'postcolonial' and the 'decolonial' both draw from many intersecting sources such as the anti-colonial thought of Aime Cesaire, C. L. R. James and Frantz Fanon, but also 'anticolonialism and postcolonialism are not progressively successive theoretical strategies, one providing better answers to questions addressed by the other',[68] and neither can postcolonialism and decoloniality be thought of in that manner. There is no linearity and teleological narrative to the 'development' of these discourses. The focus then should be on what questions they aimed to answer and what questions they are asking presently. Thus, there are a series of inquiries one can make about these discourses such as what is the point '(the *conceptual* no less than the *polemical* point)' in constructing this particular picture of colonialism or Europe at this particular time?', to which image does this 'particular picture of colonialism or Europe constitutes an answer' to, and what 'conception of colonialism or Europe is mobilized as part of a particular move'.[69]

For example, there are certain absences and presences that can be underlined to demonstrate that questions asked and the contexts in which they are asked become crucial in determining the roads taken by these theoretical discourses. Young points out the absence of Gandhi in postcolonial texts, whose writings are unlike those of Frantz Fanon and 'not a sine qua non of postcolonial readers and anthologies', which can be attributed to Gandhi's 'spiritualization of politics' and the way in which the 'division between the material and the spiritual operates within postcolonial studies'.[70] In that vein, the presence of Frantz Fanon can also be questioned. The way in which Frantz Fanon, Paulo Freire and Jose Maria Sison were received in the West and their visibility within universities demonstrate a striking absence of Sison and presence of Fanon.[71] This is not to state that Frantz Fanon should not be present, but to reiterate Stuart Hall's question, 'Why Fanon? Why Now? Why Black Skin, White Masks'.[72] Another question could be, 'Why not Sison?' The different trajectories of these figures identify 'the limitations of postcolonial studies as a critical practice in the West' and are 'tied to the containment of the symbolic currency of decolonization in American universities where globalization dominates'.[73] This absence and presence then should lead one to question the genealogies of postcolonial studies and what has been privileged in its self-narrations. Sison's disappearance reflects 'the precepts of the contemporary political establishment' as he was a 'terrorist to bureaucrats in Washington'.[74] It should also be underlined that the disappearance of his work is also related to him embodying the colonial past of the United States. These ruminations are not to discount the work of one figure in favour of another but to underline that the 'academic disciplines' have worked to construct a canon for both postcolonial studies and decoloniality, and there are presences and absences in these narratives that not only disrupt the linearity of the story but also makes one question the situatedness of these theoretical discourses in 'academic fields'.

There is no linearity that can be applied to the development of the criticisms of Eurocentrism. Furthermore, the story itself becomes more complicated when not only different geopolitics of knowledge but also different academic spaces are included. The aim of the chapter was to discuss the ways in which criticism of Eurocentrism manifests in and through disciplinary formations and geopolitics of knowledge. Thus, as the story of Eurocentrism manifests itself in and through disciplinary formations so does the criticism of Eurocentrism, and neither story should be bounded within disciplinary formations but rather thought of in and through them. Chapter 5 looks at 'postcolonial' discourses within International Relations and how criticism of Eurocentrism manifested itself within a field of study.

NOTES

1. Ania Loomba, *Colonialism/Postcolonialism* (London: Routledge, 2015); Crystal Bartolovich and Neil Lazarus, *Marxism, Modernity and Postcolonial Studies* (Cambridge: Cambridge University Press, 2002); Leela Gandhi, *Postcolonial Theory: A Critical Introduction* (New York: Columbia University Press, 1998).

2. Neil Lazarus, 'What Postcolonial Theory Doesn't Say', *Race & Class* 53, no. 1 (2011), 6.

3. Anne McClintock, 'The Angel of Progress: Pitfalls of the Term "Post-Colonialism"', *Social Text*, no. 31/32 (1992): 84–98; Ella Shohat, 'Notes on the "Post-Colonial"', *Social Text*, no. 31/32 (1992): 99–113; Vijay Mishra and Bob Hodge, 'What Is Post (-) Colonialism?', *Textual Practice* 5, no. 3 (1991): 399–414.

4. Shohat, 'Notes on the "Post-Colonial"', 104.

5. McClintock, 'The Angel of Progress: Pitfalls of the Term "Post-Colonialism"', 85.

6. Robert Young, *Postcolonialism: An Historical Introduction* (Oxford: Blackwell, 2001), 383.

7. Edward Said, *Orientalism* (New York: Vitage Books, 1978), 3.

8. Young, *Postcolonialism: An Historical Introduction*, 384.

9. Edward W. Said, 'Orientalism Reconsidered', *Cultural Critique*, no. 1 (1985), 15.

10. Anouar Abdel-Malek, 'Orientalism in Crisis', *Diogenes* 11, no. 44 (1963): 103–140; A. L. Tibawi, *English-Speaking Orientalists: A Critique of Their Approach to Islam and Arab Nationalism* (Geneva: Islamic Centre, 1965).

11. Gyan Prakash, 'Orientalism Now', *History and Theory* 34 (1995), 205.

12. 'Orientalism Now', 205.

13. Aijaz Ahmad, *In Theory: Classes, Nations, Literatures* (London: Verso, 1994).

14. Homi K. Bhabha, *The Location of Culture* (London: Routledge, 2012), 70–71.

15. *The Location of Culture*, 89.

16. Gayatri Chakravorty Spivak, 'Three Women's Texts and a Critique of Imperialism', *Critical Inquiry* 12, no. 1 (1985), 251.

17. Discussions of Spivak underline another 'category' in discussing the development of postcolonial studies: postcolonial feminism. Postcolonial feminism, or what can also be called the Third World feminism, is far from a unified group, and there are different strands within it that at times disagree with each other as well. The main starting point of the criticism towards both postcolonial studies and Western feminism is that the category of the woman needs to be included within the analysis of the postcolonial situation. Furthermore, the universal category of 'woman' in the name of which Western feminism rallies ignored the experiences of the Third World women. For further discussions on these, see Sara Suleri, 'Woman Skin Deep: Feminism and the Postcolonial Condition', *Critical Inquiry* 18, no. 4 (1992): 755–760; Narayan, 'Essence of Culture and a Sense of History: A Feminist Critique of Cultural Essentialism'; Chandra Talpade Mohanty, 'Under Western Eyes: Feminist Scholarship and Colonial Discourses', *Feminist Review*, no. 30 (1988): 61–88; '"Under Western Eyes" Revisited: Feminist Solidarity through Anticapitalist Struggles', *Signs* 28, no. 2 (2003): 499–535.

18. Ranajit Guha, ed. *Subaltern Studies, I-IV* (New Delhi: Oxford University Press, 1981–1989).

19. 'On Some Aspects of the Historiography of Colonial India', in *Mapping Subaltern Studies and the Postcolonial*, ed. Vinayak Chaturvedi (London: Verso Books, 2012), 2.

20. Arif Dirlik, 'The Postcolonial Aura: Third World Criticism in the Age of Global Capitalism', *Critical Inquiry* 20, no. 2 (1994), 302.

21. Dipesh Chakrabarty, 'Postcoloniality and the Artifice of History: Who Speaks for "Indian" Pasts?', *Representations*, no. 37 (1992), 16.

22. Florencia E. Mallon, 'The Promise and Dilemma of Subaltern Studies: Perspectives from Latin American History', *The American Historical Review* 99, no. 5 (1994), 1498.

23. Robert J. C. Young, *Colonial Desire: Hybridity in Theory, Culture and Race* (London: Routledge, 2005), 154.

24. Bart Moore Gilbert, *Postcolonial Theory* (London & New York: Verso, 1997), 4.

25. Bart Moore Gilbert, *Postcolonial Theory* (London & New York: Verso, 1997), 4.

26. The absence of postcolonial theory in French intellectual discourse is analysed by Robert Stam and Ella Shohat, 'French Intellectuals and the Postcolonial', *Interventions* 14, no. 1 (2012): 83–119.

27. Frederick Cooper, 'Conflict and Cooperation: Rethinking Colonial African History', 1518.

28. Frederick Cooper, 'Conflict and Cooperation: Rethinking Colonial African History', 1518.

29. For an engagement with subaltern studies from an Africanist perspective, see Terence Ranger, 'Subaltern Studies and "Social History"', *Southern African Review of Books* 3 (1990).

30. Cited in Toyin Falola, *Nationalism and African Intellectuals* (Rochester, NY: University Rochester Press, 2001), 235.

31. Falola, *Nationalism and African Intellectuals*, 235.

32. Walter Rodney, *How Europe Underdeveloped Africa* (Washington: Howard University Press, 1974); Rupert Lewis, *Walter Rodney's Intellectual and Political Thought* (Detroit: Wayne State University Press, 1998).

33. Andrew Coulson, *Tanzania: A Political Economy* (Oxford: Oxford University Press, 2013), 271.

34. *Tanzania: A Political Economy*, 272.

35. Michael Aronna, José Oviedo and John Beverley, eds. *The Postmodernism Debate in Latin America* (Durham and London: Duke University Press, 1995).

36. John Beverley and Jose Oviedo, 'Introduction', in *The Postmodernism Debate in Latin America*, ed. Michael Aronna and Jose Oviedo (Durham and London: Duke University Press, 1995), 9.

37. Anibal Quijano, 'Modernity, Identity, and Utopia in Latin America', in *The Postmodernism Debate in Latin America*, ed. Michael Aronna, John Beverley and Jose Oviedo (Durham and London: Duke University Press, 1995), 201.

38. 'Modernity, Identity, and Utopia in Latin America'.

39. 'Modernity, Identity, and Utopia in Latin America', 212.

40. Latin American Subaltern Studies Group, 'Founding Statement', in *The Postmodernism Debate in Latin America*, ed. Michael Aronna, John Beverley and Jose Oviedo (Durham and London: Duke University Press, 1995).

41. 'Founding Statement', 144.

42 Patricia Seed, 'Colonial and Postcolonial Discourse', *Latin American Research Review* 26, no. 3 (1991).

43. Hernan Vidal, 'The Concept of Colonial and Postcolonial Discourse: A Perspective from Literary Criticism', *Latin American Research Review* 28, no. 3 (1993); Walter D. Mignolo, 'Colonial and Postcolonial Discourse: Cultural Critique or Academic Colonialism?', *Latin American Research Review* 28, no. 3 (1993); Rolena Adorno, 'Reconsidering Colonial Discourse for Sixteenth- and Seventeenth-Century Spanish America', *Latin American Research Review* 28, no. 3 (1993); Seed, 'More Colonial and Postcolonial Discourses'.

44. 'Colonial and Postcolonial Discourse', 198.

45. Mignolo, 'Colonial and Postcolonial Discourse: Cultural Critique or Academic Colonialism?', 126.

46. Pal Ahluwalia, 'Out of Africa: Post-Structuralism's Colonial Roots', *Postcolonial Studies* 8, no. 2 (2005); *Out of Africa: Post-Structuralism's Colonial Roots* (London and New York: Routledge, 2010); Alina Sajed, *Postcolonial Encounters*

in International Relations: The Politics of Transgression in the Maghreb (London: Routledge, 2013); Robert Young, *White Mythologies: Writing History and the West* (Florence, KY: Psychology Press, 2004).

47. Rahul Rao, 'Recovering Reparative Readings of Postcolonialism and Marxism', *Critical Sociology* (2016). Another point that needs to be underlined is that Marxist thought has entered into a variety of different conversations and has been expanded upon in and through anti-colonial thought. For further studies, see Cedric J. Robinson, *Black Marxism: The Making of the Black Radical Tradition* (Chapel Hill, NC: University of North Carolina Press, 1983).

48. Young, *White Mythologies: Writing History and the West.*

49. Gandhi, *Postcolonial Theory: A Critical Introduction*, 73.

50. Ramón Grosfoguel, 'Decolonizing Post-Colonial Studies and Paradigms of Political Economy: Transmodernity, Decolonial Thinking, and Global Coloniality', Transmodernity 1, no. 1 (2011).

51. Grosfoguel, 'Decolonizing Post-Colonial Studies and Paradigms of Political Economy: Transmodernity, Decolonial Thinking, and Global Coloniality'.

52. Walter Mignolo, *Local Histories/Global Designs: Coloniality, Subaltern Knowledges, and Border Thinking*, Princeton Studies in Culture/Power/History (Princeton, NJ: Princeton University Press, 2000).

53. *The Darker Side of Western Modernity : Global Futures, Decolonial Options*, Latin America Otherwise: Languages, Empires, Nations (Durham: Duke University Press, 2011), 1.

54. Aníbal Quijano, 'Coloniality and Modernity/Rationality', *Cultural studies* 21, no. 2–3 (2007), 168.

55. 'Coloniality and Modernity/Rationality', 168.

56. Ramón Grosfoguel, 'The Epistemic Decolonial Turn: Beyond Political-Economy Paradigms', *Cultural Studies* 21, no. 2–3 (2007), 220.

57. Nelson Maldonado-Torres, 'On the Coloniality of Being: Contributions to the Development of a Concept', *Cultural Studies* 21, no. 2–3 (2007), 242.

58. 'On the Coloniality of Being: Contributions to the Development of a Concept', 257.

59. Maria Lugones, 'Heterosexualism and the Colonial/Modern Gender System', *Hypatia* 22, no. 1 (2007), 186.

60. 'Heterosexualism and the Colonial/Modern Gender System', 190.

61. Edward W. Said, *The World, the Text, and the Critic* (Cambridge, MA: Harvard University Press, 1983), 226.

62. *The World, the Text, and the Critic.*

63. Mignolo, *Local Histories/Global Designs : Coloniality, Subaltern Knowledges, and Border Thinking*, 173.

64. *Local Histories/Global Designs: Coloniality, Subaltern Knowledges, and Border Thinking.*

65. *Local Histories/Global Designs: Coloniality, Subaltern Knowledges, and Border Thinking*, 175.

66. Walter D. Mignolo, 'Delinking: The Rhetoric of Modernity, the Logic of Coloniality and the Grammar of De-Coloniality 1', *Cultural Studies* 21, no. 2–3 (2007), 498.

67. Benita Parry, *Postcolonial Studies: A Materialist Critique* (London: Routledge, 2004), 13.

68. David Scott, 'The Social Construction of Postcolonial Studies', in *Postcolonial Studies and Beyond*, ed. Ania Looma, et al. (Durham, NC: Duke University Press, 2005), 391.

69. 'The Social Construction of Postcolonial Studies', 398.

70. Young, *Postcolonialism: An Historical Introduction*, 337.

71. Charlie Samuya Veric, 'Third World Project, or How Poco Failed', *Social Text* 31, no. 1 (2013), 114.

72. Stuart Hall, 'The after-Life of Frantz Fanon: Why Fanon? Why Now? Why Black Skin, White Masks?', in *The Fact of Blackness: Frantz Fanon and Visual Representation*, ed. Alan Read. (Seattle, WA: Bay Press,1996). Also see, Henry Louis Gates Jr., 'Critical Fanonism', *Critical Inquiry* 17, no. 3 (1991): 457–70; Cedric Robinson, 'The Appropriation of Frantz Fanon', *Race & Class* 35, no.1 (1993): 79–91.

73. Veric, 'Third World Project, or How Poco Failed'.

74. 'Third World Project, or How Poco Failed'.

Chapter 5

Constructing the Non-Western

The aim of this chapter is to trace the way theoretical strategies criticizing Eurocentrism entered into conversation with the disciplinary formation of International Relations (IR). The first part of the chapter discusses the questions that were asked of IR and postcolonial theory and the points of conversation. The second and third parts of the chapter will focus on the different manifestations of the criticism of Eurocentrism within IR: the second part on how the non-West was brought into accounts of the international and the third part on how the non-West was brought into discussions of IR. The fourth part of the chapter will focus on the issues related to bringing in the non-West into stories of the international and IR.

The way in which IR as a 'discipline' has dealt with the issue of questioning Eurocentrism will be the focus of this chapter. David Scott asks a pertinent question with respect to postcolonial studies and the questions that informed it at its inception and whether or not these questions continue to be the questions that still need to be asked or do new questions need to be formulated for our new postcolonial present.[1] This is an important question to bear in mind in general when approaching the questions of 'theories', 'disciplines' and 'concepts'. As Said states, 'Texts are wordly, to some degree they are events,' and they are 'part of the social world, human life, and of course the historical movements in which they are located and interpreted'.[2] Thus, 'texts have ways of existing, both theoretical and practical, that even in their most rarefied form are always enmeshed in circumstance, time, place, and society – in short, they are in the world, and hence are wordly'.[3] Furthermore, 'a critic may often be, but is not merely, the alchemical translator of texts into circumstantial reality or worldliness; for he too is subject to and a producer of circumstances, and these are felt regardless of whatever objectivity his method possesses'.[4]

The worldliness of the text and the critic points to the intertwined histories of concepts and theories, travelling theories as issues to be underlined. The connectedness of the theories and the different influences and histories that they stem from has been discussed in Chapter 4. The aim of Chapter 4 was to highlight the conversations and intertwined histories that existed in and through such categories as postcolonial, decolonial and anti-colonial thought. The reading and writing of these theories in international relations is the focus of this chapter. There is then in the 'entry' into IR, the question of how these theories became connected into IR and how that travel occurred. The question then becomes following from David Scott's[5] formulation through the terminology, what questions were 'postcolonial IR' aiming to answer and how much do these questions actually inform our postcolonial present.

ENGAGING INTERNATIONAL RELATIONS

The main discussion point, as discussed in Chapter 4, with respect to post-colonial studies has been its relationship with poststructuralism. One of the main ways in which postcolonial studies entered into IR has been as a corrective to the critical perspectives on IR. Sankaran Krishna's review essay, 'The Importance of Being Ironic: A Postcolonial View on Critical International Relations Theory',[6] is in this sense an important starting point to locate the postcolonial criticism to critical international relations theory. In this article, Krishna reviews books that today can be characterized as the main stopping points of critical IR, such as David Campbell's *Writing Security*[7] and James Der Derian's *Antidiplomacy*.[8] His criticism is informed by a postcolonial perspective which entails

> a sensitivity to the hierarchical relations between races, genders, and classes; the ethnocentricity of a discipline that, by definition and nomenclature (international relations), should emphasize the historical and interrelated character of developments over the last few centuries; who controls the dominant discourses of our times; and the role of critical international theory in the endless plays of power.[9]

Looking at the writings of critical IR through the postcolonial perspective, Krishna underlines the self-referential view of the West and how critical perspectives 'are oblivious to the intimate dialogue between "Western" and "non-Western" economies, societies, and philosophies that underwrite the disenchantment with modernity that characterizes the present epoch'.[10] Through his reading of critical perspectives on international relations, Krishna opens space up for postcolonial perspectives on international relations and how it can work as a corrective to the field of international relations.

Phillip Darby and A. J. Paolini's article on bridging international relations and postcolonialism also sets the stage in discussing how postcolonial perspectives can become part of IR. They argue that postcolonial discourse focuses 'on the relations of domination and resistance and the effect they have had on identity, in, through, and beyond the colonial encounter'.[11] In their genealogies and trajectories of postcolonial discourse, Darby and Paolini point to different ways in which postcolonialism and international relations can enter into conversations. The first point of conversation they underline is, 'similar interests in culture, identity, representation and narrative', mainly through the focus on postmodernity that frames some postcolonial discourse and the 'third debate' in international relations. Apart from the commonality of postmodernism, the authors identify three areas: imperialism, Orientalism and culture that can create dialogue between postcolonial discourse and international relations. The focus on why these concerns have not thus far wielded any dialogue demonstrates the issues with IR as a discipline. Looking at the issue of imperialism, they note that engagement with imperialism might have led IR to rethink 'international politics of the Third world or to a recognition of the cultural factors in world politics'.[12] This was caused from the disciplinary boundaries through which the international has been conceptualized and how imperial relations were not considered as an object of study. In the end, they underline that postcolonialism presents a series of challenges to IR and 'not only about its neglects of the Third World and about the way its construction of international politics distorts thinking about the Third world, but to the very epistemological basis of the discipline and its implication in a global design to serve Western interests'.[13]

These discussions about how and to what extent and in which respects postcolonial could become part of discussions within IR underlines certain points that were taken up in different respects within the field of international studies. The first is the necessity to underline the dialogue between the West and the non-West. This relates to issues of the power and knowledge nexus and bringing in empire into the stories of the international. The second is about the nature of the discipline of international relations. The ways in which the 'postcolonial' can enter into conversations with international relations as a corrective to the 'centred' nature of the discipline.[14] The way in which the concerns of postcolonial studies entered into the discipline as such is about the 'centredness' of the discipline and how to 'decentre' it. As Branwen Gruffydd Jones states:

> International Relations (IR) scholarship and teaching has remained concerned predominantly with relations between and issues of concern to the great powers,

the hegemons, the large and powerful in the global political economy. The standard historical reference points of the discipline's rendering of international relations are drawn almost exclusively from Europe's 'internal' history. The acknowledged disciplinary canon of modern IR consists of European classical thought. For much of the twentieth century and into the twenty-first, the field of IR has been dominated by North American, European, and to a lesser extent Australian scholars. Thus, the majority of literature in the discipline of IR is written by and about only some of the peoples of the world – predominantly Americans and Europeans. IR remains guilty of forgetting and detracting from the thought and acts of not only the people of Africa but also the 'rest' of the non-Western world.[15]

The absence of the non-Western world from understanding of the international has been one of the main focus points about the works that attempted to bring in postcolonial perspectives in dialogue with IR. The next section will discuss the works that aim to question the absence of non-West within IR.

NON-WEST IN THE INTERNATIONAL

The stories of the international had predominantly focused on the 'Western' story of the international and as such concepts through which international relations were made intelligible, such as the international system, Westphalian sovereignty and security, reflected an absence of the non-West. Stories of international relations, the international society and IR theory are based upon a story that has Europe at its centre, a story that edits out the disruptions and constructs a linear unproblematized tale of the 'rise of the West', 'the expansion of International society' and 'the origins of the state system'. The stories might have different titles and might prioritize different aspects – the story of security, the story of the state, the story of the international – yet the periodizations, the events and setting are dependent upon a specific understanding of European history.

The Eurocentric account of the international system is constitutive of the field and defines the boundaries of the discourse on IR. The silences and omissions from the story of the development of the international system condition the manner in which concepts such as security and sovereignty are defined. As such, retelling the story as it has been told reproduces the implicit hierarchies inscribed within the narrative. As Seth states, 'Any satisfactory account of the emergence of the modern international system cannot simply chart how an international society that developed in the West radiated outwards, but rather seek to explore the ways in which international society was shaped by the interactions between Europe and those it colonized'.[16]

These omissions have been questioned from a wide range of perspectives that have been informed by the postcolonial discourses of the underlying absence of the non-West from the study of the international, though that might not necessarily be categorized as subscribing to 'postcolonial theory'.

The processes, structures and actors privileged by a Eurocentric understanding of the international system delineate events that do not 'fit' within the definitions of these structures and actors as part of the story. For example, characterizing the period from 1815 to 1914 as peaceful requires ignoring a series of wars, mutinies and conquests. But they do not 'count' and hence cannot disrupt the 'Hundred Years Peace' because 'wars are defined exclusively as the acts of sovereign powers on each other', and, as a result, 'the Revolt of 1857 that swept across northern India, that resulted in tens of thousands of deaths, and that at one point looked likely to bring a forcible end to the British Raj there does not count', rather it becomes 'a mere "Mutiny" ... a "domestic" issue by its very definition incapable of altering the Hundred Years' Peace'.[17] A similar construction of a period of peace is made with respect to the Cold War in referring to it as the 'Long Peace',[18] focusing on the fact that the two superpowers did not directly engage in war, yet it completely ignores the violent independence wars in the Third World.

Events that do not 'fit' into the linear narrative and have been edited out in order to centre Europe have also been brought into the story. The narrative of the 'Age of Revolutions' centres upon the French and American revolutions, and 'Haiti was purposefully forgotten from historical memory as something unimaginable, unintelligible and unthinkable'.[19] Taking the Haitian Revolution out of the narrative of revolutions that paved the way for the establishment of the present understanding of human rights presents it as originating only from the West when 'the Haitian Revolution properly belongs to the genealogy of modern conceptions of constitutional power, popular sovereignty and entitlements for the citizenry'.[20] As with the story of the expansion of the international system, the travels of state and sovereignty cannot be narrated independent of imperialism, since 'imperialism in its many forms was essential in shaping the character of both Europe and the non-European world; it is their common history'.[21] Neither state nor sovereignty remained fixed as it developed within Europe and neither did they travel in a linear unproblematic manner to the non-Europeans. Imperialism was an important part of the multitude of stories of state and sovereignty in and outside of Europe.

The story of the way in which state and sovereignty expanded to establish the international system assumed not only the unilinearity of the process but also that it happened in an unproblematic manner. It also assumed that the decolonization process happened within the contours of international law ignoring that the story of international law and the codification of the rights of states and the extent of their sovereignty was also shaped by imperialism. As Anghie argues, 'Sovereignty is formulated in such a way as to exclude the non-European; following which, sovereignty can then be deployed to identify, locate, sanction and transform the uncivilized'.[22] The story of the manner in which sovereignty and state travelled is predicated on a story of international law that is itself Eurocentric, and its decisions with respect to who gets to be a state and who has sovereignty privileges the European definition and imposes the 'ideal' set in Europe to be the aim. The 'sovereignty doctrine expels the non-European world from its realm, and then proceeds to legitimise the imperialism that resulted in the incorporation of the non-European world into the system of international law'.[23] As a result of these dynamics, telling the story through the prism of international law and standards established by European states turns the story of the decolonization process and the postcolonial state to one of its lack, weakness and failure. Thus, the postcolonial state is always in a process of trying to fulfil the main tenets of international law that will enable its joining of the Westphalian international system.

The multitude of stories of decolonization and postcolonial state formation cannot be told without pointing out that 'sovereignty regimes reflect historical distributions of power and subjectivity within the international order and corresponding symbolic and material economies'.[24] In that vein, Grovogui brings forth the story of Namibia's decolonization, demonstrating how 'the UN debate concerning Namibia was driven primarily by the desire of Western nations to maintain the existing hierarchies of the international order and the attempt by Third World nations to subvert those structures'.[25] Through the story of Namibia, Grovogui challenges the story of the 'failed state' by looking at 'who failed the "failed state"'?[26] Shilliam questions the 'historical narrative that assumed an unprecedented transformation of sovereignty from a (putatively) Westphalian territorial principle to a post-Westphalian extra-territorial principle'.[27] Thus, he brings forth the story of Marcus Garvey and the Universal Negro Improvement Association (UNIA)[28] to demonstrate that the linear unproblematized passage from Westphalia to post-Westphalian order in Europe also needs to be problematized. The example of UNIA, in which 'sovereignty was expressed through a political subject that took the form of an impersonal Pan-African collective',[29] disrupts the story of the end of Westphalia that has come with the European Union. Shilliam also points out that 'a number of trans-national and/or extra-territorial political and intellectual currents drove the political upheavals surrounding World War I',[30] hence problematizing the narrative of the development of the state in Europe and its passage to a post-Westphalian order in the post-Cold War period. Even if these movements were unsuccessful, 'rather than being rendered invisible or as curiosities in a uni-linear narrative, the existence of the "marginal" alternatives presented at the *fin-de-siecle* and their cumulative lived experiences should be taken as constitutive of the pre-existing and ongoing multi-linear transformation of sovereignty in the modern epoch'.[31]

The works that have brought the non-West in have been important in questioning the main narratives that constitute the international but have also worked to direct the focus on the non-West as a problem that needs to be solved.

INTERNATIONAL RELATIONS IN THE NON-WEST

The second arena in which the non-West has been brought in has been the discipline of IR and understandings for which knowledge is produced. There have been a myriad of works focusing on different trajectories of IR within the non-West, non-Western IR and non-Western thought.[32] The starting point of the 'geocultural epistemologies'[33] project was precisely to inquire that the 'IR in different settings, both as scholarship in its own right and within the framework of a critical understanding of the discipline as a whole, would deepen our comprehension of and receptivity to knowledge produced around the world'.[34] The case studies have been wide ranging, focusing on China,[35] India,[36] Japan,[37] Russia[38] and Turkey. The geocultural epistemologies' project increases our knowledge of the different ways in which IR as an institutional entity has developed in different contexts.

One common strand in the discussions focusing on the different IRs that exist in the world is the underlying of how theory is used. The general division between 'theory-testing' and 'theory-building' becomes an important discussion point. Mallavarapu laments that in India 'theory is still fundamentally a marginal enterprise'.[39] Within this framework, the questions asked of the non-Western setting are about their 'lack of theory' and about how to make the 'non-West' speak to the theoretical establishment of the 'West'. As Chan states, the '(emerging) non-Western IRT in Asia can be understood as a "derivative discourse[40]" of the modern West reproducing the logic of colonial modernity rather than disrupting it', treating 'East and West as oppositional entities'.[41] Furthering this problem is 'the way non-Western IR is promoted in the discipline', which has cast 'the "burden of proof" onto those IR scholars who live and work in the non-Western periphery rather than propel those who do Western IR to reflect upon the epistemological/political implications of their approach and to communicate with the former'.[42] Moreover, the categories of the 'West' and the 'non-West' also obscure the ways in which there may be 'elements of "non-Western" experiences and ideas built in to those ostensibly "Western" approaches to the study of world politics' and 'what we think of as "non-Western" approaches to world politics may be suffused with "Western" concepts and theories'.[43]

The third instalment of the 'geocultural epistemologies' project recognizes some of these problems and includes within itself reflexive contributions about the 'state of IR' and the road ahead.[44] Tickner and Blainey argue that exploring geocultural difference may 'prove too limited in that it accepts as its own point of departure the very ideas that are at the root of the modern Western worldview'.[45] Furthermore, they state:

> These books indicate that, generally speaking, plurality in global IR is one that evolves within a (narrow) space allowed for by the United States and Western European core, which exercises a strong disciplining function in terms of the theories, concepts, and categories authorized to count as knowledge of world politics. We worry that our original premise, that achieving greater dialogue and pluralism within the field requires making visible scholarly work that has either gone unacknowledged as a legitimate contribution to knowledge or that has occupied subordinate positions, may potentially leave disciplinary foundations and power asymmetries intact, when in fact our underlying goal has been to promote their transformation.[46]

The search for IR, IRT and theory in the non-West privileges these terms and continues to reproduce the disciplinary boundaries because the search works in looking for them through the criteria that have been established by Western academia in general and the discipline of IR in particular.

TRAVELS AND TRIBULATIONS OF THE NON-WEST

This section aims to elaborate on the issues associated with turning the non-West into a problem to be solved rather than IR. Uma Narayan[47] and Chandra Mohanty[48] criticize the categories of 'women', 'Western women' and 'Third World women', and these discussions demonstrate the issues with constructing the non-West as the problematic subject of IR. The construction of the Western and non-Western difference was part of the mechanisms that reproduced colonial differences. Thus, what is taken to be 'Western culture' only had 'a faint resemblance to the moral, political, cultural values that *actually pervaded* life in Western societies', and, as such, the notions of liberty and equality were constructed as Western values even when 'Western nations were engaged in slavery, colonization, expropriation, and the denial of liberty and equality not only to the colonized but to large segments of Western subjects, including women'.[49] Furthermore, there existed similarities between the 'Western culture' and its Others, 'such as hierarchical social systems, huge economic disparities between members, and the mistreatments and inequality of women'. Thus, in the construction of Western and non-Western, for example, spirituality became a characteristic of the non-West, which became embraced by nationalists in their anticolonialist arguments.[50] These sharply differentiated ideas of the 'cultures' became reproduced, and both sides 'failed to register the degree to which their very constitution as "Western" or "non-Western" subjects resulted from the putative contrasts between "cultures"'[51]. As such, the issue of the non-West and its difference in relation to the West is a construction that works to privilege the West but also continues to create the non-West as a problem to be solved.

The acceptance and reproduction of this difference also works to maintain the idea that 'equality', 'human rights' and 'democracy' belong to 'Western culture', but in reality rather than belonging to the West, these doctrines developed in 'struggles *against Western imperialism*'.[52] Furthermore, it needs to be underlined 'that a value or practice's being "Non-western" (either in terms of its origin or its context of prevalence) does not mean that is is anti-imperialist or anti-colonial'.[53] This elaboration points to many non-West and postcolonial states that continue the practices of exclusion along the axis of class and gender and hide behind the cloak of non-Western values. As such, the 'reflexivity' of the 'Western' interlocutors is rooted in their 'designation of the other as a barrier' that confirms the 'impenetrability of the other' and continues to trap one 'within the confines of the colonial encounter'.[54] Moreover, the non-West entering the story of the international works to reproduce the issues of IR in flattening out the 'international' into bounded entities which work to silence the myriad of issues and concepts within the non-West.[55]

The constructions of the non-West enable an arena in which being situated in the non-West brings forth criticism of the international system. This position is privileged such that the Western interlocutor silences themselves in the name of reflexivity that creates the 'other' and its own privileged position in being able to designate an other. Furthermore, this assignment of the non-West works to privilege the 'ruling party' and the 'dominant narrative' in the non-West that works to ignore the class, gendered, racial and intellectual hierarchies at work which are not less complicated than those in the West. As Muppidi asks, 'How does one, raised on the vices of colonialism and the virtues of freedom, nationalism and independence'[56] relate to and make sense of the violence of the postcolonial state. Furthermore, he asks, 'What failure of form, what failure of the postcolonial, lies here?'[57] The arguments of this section have been to underline that the concern with the non-West as a category to be brought in has been a consequence of the ways in which the theoretical strategies criticizing Eurocentrism were translated into the disciplinary formation of IR. IR as a disciplinary formation was constructed in and through difference which allowed 'us to claim to "solve" the problem by negotiating a modus vivendi among political communities', yet the problem remained whereby 'the bounded political community constructs (and is constructed by) the other.[58] As such, it is not just the locus of enunciation with respect to geopolitics of knowledge that needs to be underlined but also the audience and disciplinary formations being addressed. In that sense, 'It is as much the saying (and the audience involved) as what is said (and the world referred to) that preserve or transform the image of the real constructed by previous acts of saying and previous utterances'.[59] This means that criticism of Eurocentrism manifested itself in a certain way within IR because of the disciplinary formations of the field and the privileged concerns it had.

CONCLUSION

The aim of the chapter has been to discuss the ways in which criticisms of Eurocentrism have manifested themselves within the field of IR. The first part of the chapter discussed the main ways in which postcolonial concerns made their way into the disciplinary formation of IR. The second and third parts of the chapter focused on how the non-West was brought into IR. The second part focused on how the story of the non-West was brought into the story of the 'international'. The third part focused on works that dealt with IR in the non-West. The fourth part discussed the issues related to navigating the non-West and the opportunities it brought and the limitations it imposed. The aim of the chapter has been to elaborate on the manifestations of the criticism of Eurocentrism within the disciplinary formation of IR and to underline that looking for the non-West and Eurocentrism within the boundaries of the discipline overlooks the fact that the absence of the non-West is '*constitutive* both of the discipline and of subjects and objects of security in different parts of the world'.[60] This historical absence cannot be remedied only through including the non-Western or making the non-Western more present, it needs to go 'beyond adding and stirring'.[61] The absence of the non-West is not like the missing piece of a puzzle, which if we are able to locate will finally 'solve' the puzzle. Thus, the purpose is not to add the non-West into the present 'archive of Western academy, for that is a continuation in the intellectual sphere of imperial expansion and colonial rule', but rather 'the purpose is to undermine the security of an epistemological cartography that quarantines legitimate knowledge production of modernity to one (idealized) geo-cultural site'.[62] This is not to downplay the importance of the works that have been done but that moving from David Scott's formulation our postcolonial present necessitates new questions,[63] questions that do not present the non-West as a problem to be solved but rather IR as the problem to be tackled. As such, the question is how to 're-write' international relations rather than how to write the non-West into international relations.

NOTES

1. Scott, 'The Social Construction of Postcolonial Studies'.

2. Said, *The World, the Text, and the Critic*, 4.

3. *The World, the Text, and the Critic*, 4.

4. *The World, the Text, and the Critic*, 4.

5. Scott, 'The Social Construction of Postcolonial Studies'.

6. Sankaran Krishna, 'The Importance of Being Ironic: A Postcolonial View on Critical International Relations Theory', *Alternatives* 18, no. 3 (1993): 385–417.

7. David Campbell, *Writing Security : United States Foreign Policy and the Politics of Identity* (Minneapolis: University of Minnesota Press, 1998).

8. James Der Derian, *Antidiplomacy: Spies, Terror, Speed and War* (Cambridge: Blackwell Publishers, 1992).

9. Krishna, 'The Importance of Being Ironic: A Postcolonial View on Critical International Relations Theory', 390.

10. 'The Importance of Being Ironic: A Postcolonial View on Critical International Relations Theory', 388.

11. Phillip Darby and Albert J. Paolini, 'Bridging International Relations and Post-colonialism', *Alternatives: Global, Local, Political* 19, no. 3 (1994), 375.

12. 'Bridging International Relations and Postcolonialism', 380.

13. 'Bridging International Relations and Postcolonialism', 394.

14. Meghana Nayak and Eric Selbin, *Decentering International Relations* (London; New York: Zed, 2010).

15. Branwen Gruffydd Jones, 'Introduction: International Relations, Eurocentrism, and Imperialism', in *Decolonizing International Relations*, ed. Branwen Gruffydd Jones (Lanham, MD: Rowman & Littlefield, 2006), 1–2.

16. Seth, 'Postcolonial Theory and the Critique of International Relations', 174.

17. Krishna, 'Race, Amnesia, and the Education of International Relations', 404–405.

18. John Lewis Gaddis, 'The Long Peace: Elements of Stability in the Post-War International System', *International Security* 10, no. 4 (1986): 99–142.

19. Robbie Shilliam, 'Civilization and the Poetics of Slavery', *Thesis Eleven* 108, no. 1 (2012), 100.

20. Grovogui, 'Mind, Body, and Gut! Elements of a Postcolonial Human Rights Discourse', 186.

21. Tarak Barkawi and Mark Laffey, 'Retrieving the Imperial: Empire and International Relations', *Millennium-Journal of International Studies* 31, no. 1 (2002), 113.

22. Anghie, *Imperialism, Sovereignty and the Making of International Law*, 37, 311.

23. 'The Evolution of International Law: Colonial and Postcolonial Realities', *Third World Quarterly* 27, no. 5 (2006), 739.

24. Siba Grovogui, 'Regimes of Sovereignty: International Morality and the African Condition', *European Journal of International Relations* 8, no. 3 (2002), 328.

25. Grovogui, Sovereigns, *Quasi Sovereigns, and Africans: Race and Self-Determination in International Law*, 184.

26. Pınar Bilgin and Adam David Morton, 'Historicising Representations Of "failed States": Beyond the Cold-War Annexation of the Social Sciences?', *Third World Quarterly* 23, no. 1 (2002): 55–80.

27. Shilliam, 'What About Marcus Garvey? Race and the Transformation of Sovereignty Debate'.

28. Universal Negro Improvement Association.

29. Shilliam, 'What About Marcus Garvey? Race and the Transformation of Sovereignty Debate', 397.

30. 'What About Marcus Garvey? Race and the Transformation of Sovereignty Debate', 381.

31. 'What About Marcus Garvey? Race and the Transformation of Sovereignty Debate', 400.

32. Acharya and Buzan, *Non-Western International Relations Theory: Perspectives on and Beyond Asia*; Shilliam, *International Relations and Non-Western Thought: Imperialism, Colonialism and Investigations of Global Modernity*.

33. Arlene B. Tickner and Ole Wæver, eds. *International Relations Scholarship around the World* (London: Routledge, 2009); Tickner and Blaney, *Thinking International Relations Differently*; *Claiming the International* (London: Routledge, 2013).

34. Ole Waever and Arlene B. Tickner, 'Introduction: Geocultural Epistemologies', in *International Relations Scholarship around the World*, ed. Ole Waever and Arlene B. Tickner (London: Routledge, 2009), 2.

35. Qin Yaqing, 'Why Is There No Chinese International Relations Theory?', *International Relations of the Asia-Pacific* 7, no. 3 (2007): 313–340.

36. Siddharth Mallavarapu, 'Development of International Relations Theory in India Traditions, Contemporary Perspectives and Trajectories', *International Studies* 46, no. 1–2 (2009): 165–183.

37. Kosuke Shimizu, 'Materializing the "Non-Western": Two Stories of Japanese Philosophers on Culture and Politics in the Inter-War Period', *Cambridge Review of International Affairs* 28, no. 1 (2015): 3–20; Takashi Inoguchi, 'Are There Any Theories of International Relations in Japan?', *International Relations of the Asia-Pacific* 7, no. 3 (2007): 369–390.

38. Andrei P. Tsygankov and Pavel A. Tsygankov, 'National Ideology and IR Theory: Three Incarnations of The "Russian Idea"', *European Journal of International Relations* 16, no.4 (2010): 663–686.

39. Mallavarapu, 'Development of International Relations Theory in India Traditions, Contemporary Perspectives and Trajectories', 180.

40. Chatterjee, Partha, *Nationalist thought and the colonial world : A derivative disccourse* (London : Zed Books, 1986).

41. Ching-Chang Chen, 'The Absence of Non-Western IR Theory in Asia Reconsidered', *International Relations of the Asia-Pacific* 11, no. 1 (2011), 5; also see, 'The Im/Possibility of Building Indigenous Theories in a Hegemonic Discipline: The Case of Japanese International Relations', *Asian Perspective* 36, no. 3 (2012): 463–492.

42. 'The Absence of Non-Western IR Theory in Asia Reconsidered', 18.

43. Pınar Bilgin, 'Thinking Past "Western" IR?', *Third World Quarterly* 29, no. 1 (2008), 5–6.

44. David L. Blaney and Arlene B. Tickner, 'Introduction: Claiming the International Beyond IR', in *Claiming the International*, ed. David L. Blaney and Arlene B. Tickner (London: Routledge, 2013); Inanna Hamati-Ataya, 'Worlding Beyond the Self? IR, the Subject, and the Cartesian Anxiety', in *Claiming the International*, ed. David L. Blaney and Arlene B. Tickner (London: Routledge, 2013); Arlene B.

Tickner, 'By Way of Conclusion: Forget IR?', in *Claiming the International*, ed. David L. Blaney and Arlene B. Tickner (London: Routledge, 2013).

45. Blaney and Tickner, 'Introduction: Claiming the International Beyond IR', 3.

46. 'Introduction: Claiming the International Beyond IR', 4.

47. Narayan, 'Essence of Culture and a Sense of History: A Feminist Critique of Cultural Essentialism'.

48. Mohanty, 'Under Western Eyes: Feminist Scholarship and Colonial Discourses'; '"Under Western Eyes" Revisited: Feminist Solidarity through Anticapitalist Struggles'.

49. Narayan, 'Essence of Culture and a Sense of History: A Feminist Critique of Cultural Essentialism', 89–90.

50. Chatterjee, Partha, *The Nation and Its Fragments : Colonial and Postcolonial Histories* (Princeton, New Jersey : Princeton University Press, 1993).

51. Narayan, 'Essence of Culture and a Sense of History: A Feminist Critique of Cultural Essentialism', 91

52. Narayan, 'Essence of Culture and a Sense of History: A Feminist Critique of Cultural Essentialism', 97.

53. 'Essence of Culture and a Sense of History: A Feminist Critique of Cultural Essentialism', 99.

54. Asha Varadharajan, *Exotic Parodies: Subjectivity in Adorno, Said, and Spivak* (Minneapolis, MN: University of Minnesota Press, 1995), xvii.

55. This point also works to underline the issue with the concomitant construction of the West and Europe that goes along with the construction of the non-West. This results in accepting the linear narrative of the European story as the only possible narrative of Europe's past but also accepts the periodizations through which that past is made intelligible, such as the medieval and modern distinction. For further information on these discussions, see Sandra Halperin, 'International Relations Theory and the Hegemony of Western Conceptions of Modernity', in *Decolonizing International Relations*, ed. Branwen Gruffydd Jones (Lanham: Rowman & Littlefield, 2006); Kathleen Davis, *Periodization and Sovereignty: How Ideas of Feudalism and Secularization Govern the Politics of Time*, The Middle Ages Series (Philadelphia: University of Pennsylvania Press, 2008).

56. Himadeep Muppidi, *Politics in Emotion: The Song of Telangana* (London: Routledge, 2014), 37.

57. *Politics in Emotion: The Song of Telangana*, 39.

58. Naeem Inayatullah and David L. Blaney, *International Relations and the Problem of Difference* (London: Routledge, 2004), 6.

59. Mignolo, 'Colonial and Postcolonial Discourse: Cultural Critique or Academic Colonialism?', 128.

60. Bilgin, 'The "Western-Centrism" of Security Studies: "Blind Spot" or Constitutive Practice?', 616.

61. 'The "Western-Centrism" of Security Studies: "Blind Spot" or Constitutive Practice?', 617.

62. Robbie Shilliam, 'The Perilous but Unavoidable Terrain of the Non-West', in *International Relations and Non-Western Thought: Imperialism, Colonialism and Investigations of Global Modernity*, ed. Robbie Shilliam (London: Routledge, 2010), 24.

63. Scott, 'The Social Construction of Postcolonial Studies'.

Conclusion

The aim of the book has been to present a possible way of reading and re-writing the Eurocentrism of International Relations. The method proposed in this book for such an endeavour is to re-write histories of the manifestations and criticisms of Eurocentrism through 'connected histories'.[1] The book has provided an example as to how to write 'connected histories' of International Relations as a discipline. The first point to be underlined has been that the aim of 'connected histories' should be to 'redraw maps that emerge from the problematics we wish to study rather than insert problematics to fit our pre-existing categories'.[2] In that sense, connected histories approach encourages us to trace the connections and geographies that emerge from these connections in writing about a problematique than to conceptualize that problematique within pre-existing boundaries of knowledge whether this be disciplinary formations or geopolitical contexts. The aim should not only be to 'compare from within our boxes, but spend some time and effort to transcend them, not by comparison alone but by seeking out the at times fragile threads that connected the globe'.[3] The aim of the book has been to present an example in this endeavour through the story of Eurocentrism in and through International Relations. The book has focused on two aspects of the story of Eurocentrism in and through International Relations. The first aspect, which was discussed in Section I, entitled 'Manifestations of Eurocentrism', focused on the ways in which Eurocentrism manifested itself in and through disciplines and geopolitical contexts. The second aspect, which was discussed in Section II, entitled 'Criticisms of Eurocentrism' focused on how criticism of Eurocentrism manifested itself in and through disciplinary formations and geopolitical knowledges.

MANIFESTATIONS OF EUROCENTRISM

Section I focused on the manifestation of Eurocentrism in and through disciplinary formations and geopolitical contexts. The section underlined the different manifestations of Eurocentrism, whether culturalist, historical or epistemic,[4] in the workings of history, historiography and 'the past' as experienced.

Chapter 1, entitled 'History' in International Relations, focused on the relationship between the disciplines of history and International Relations. It underlined that the past *as it happened* cannot be recovered and reconstructed. History as such remains a retelling that is always incomplete. Thus, bringing in history into international relations needs to account for how history itself is a problematic discipline. The chapter underlined that the 'past' and history are not the same but rather traces of the past are transformed into history. This transformation takes place based on a series of considerations such as the central subject; the geographical centre and a series of questions such as what happened next and how did it happen. These considerations are also shaped by the historiographical debate that provides the historian with the road map of what has been argued, the interpretations of events and possible future research areas. Historiography constructs the borders of the historiographical debate and centres the understanding of the past to specific concepts, events and actors by privileging them and their interpretations. Furthermore, these debates construct periods and concepts of the past whereby the discourses of the past come to be seen as if they were the past silencing other possible renditions. Thus, historiographical debates 'write' and 'make' their object of inquiry but are also limited by them.[5] As such, history is historiography because history is 'a written discourse about the past and pre-existing narratives', and, as such, 'there is no history only historiography defined as what we write about the past in order to understand it'.[6]

The focus on the 'past', history and historiography demonstrates that the relationship between international relations and history needs to take into account the problematic nature of history.[7] This means that issues discussed within International Relations and the problems posed within the discipline have to be thought of in and through their relationship with other disciplines such as history. The story of Eurocentrism within International Relations as such has to take into account the manifestations of Eurocentrism in and through disciplinary formations. Chapters 2 and 3 focus on the manifestations of Eurocentrism in and between disciplinary formations. The Eurocentrism that manifests itself is primarily historical in the sense that 'world politics is taken to be happening almost exclusively in Europe, or latterly in the Northern hemisphere', and the entry of the Third World into debates 'is derivative of European developments and driven by great-power competition and the diffusion of European ideas and institutions'.[8] Nonetheless, the writings and makings of the historiographical debate and how they function to delimit the possible and impossible should be underlined.[9] Furthermore, the characterizations and framings of who is included and the reasons behind such inclusions and exclusions also include within themselves culturalist manifestations.

Chapter 2, entitled 'International Relations in History', focused on how Eurocentrism manifests itself in historiographical debates about the Cold War and how the boundaries of these historiographical debates are reproduced in the context of Turkey. The 'writing' and 'making' of the Cold War in historiographical debate works to establish Europe and the West as the central subjects of history. The way in which historiographical debates 'write' and 'make' the Cold War also determine the borders of the 'history' that comes to be accepted as the past. Berkhofer gives the example of the blind sages describing the different parts of the elephant but all of them still describing the elephant.[10] The way in which history disciplines the past and constructs the basic tenets of historiography delimits the borders of what History is whereby historiographical debates are conditioned by the assumption that all that can be analysed is the different interpretations of the elephant, limiting and excluding the possibilities of a myriad of great stories such as the case of the Haitian Revolution.[11]

Chapter 3, entitled 'The Past as Experienced', focused on the manifestations of Eurocentrism that can be 'read' through the traces of the 'past'.[12] The chapter focused on different manifestations of Eurocentrism and the different hierarchies that were reproduced. As such, different hierarchies were reproduced between the West and Turkey in discussions about the international system, the importance and centrality of the United States, the threat of communism and the Soviet Union. The section traced the different manifestations of Eurocentrism in and through disciplines and geopolitical contexts. Tracing the manifestations of Eurocentrism in and through disciplinary formations and geopolitical contexts underscores the need for connected histories in order to tackle the issue of Eurocentrism which should not be thought of as manifesting in a linear manner within disciplinary formations. This also raises the issue of criticisms of Eurocentrism. The criticisms of Eurocentrism also do not present a uniform story but exist in and through disciplines and geopolitical knowledges. As such, criticizing Eurocentrism just as tracing Eurocentrism needs to be thought of as existing in and between disciplinary formations and geopolitical knowledges.

CRITICISMS OF EUROCENTRISM

Section II focused on criticisms of Eurocentrism in and through disciplines and geopolitical contexts. The section underlined the different ways in which theoretical strategies criticizing Eurocentrism were formulated in conversation with each other across disciplines and geopolitical contexts. It also pointed to the different conversations that continue in and between disciplines as the theoretical strategies being discussed are not rooted in one 'discipline' and move between different disciplines.

Chapter 4, entitled 'Coloniality, Postcoloniality, Decoloniality', focused on the conversations between different theoretical strategies that problematize the Eurocentrism of the social sciences and the humanities. The chapter underlined how the 'academic disciplines' have worked to construct a canon for both postcolonial studies and decolonial thought, and how there are presences and absences in these narratives that not only disrupt the linearity of the story but also makes one question the situatedness of these theoretical discourses in 'academic fields'. The tracing of the development of theoretical strategies aiming to criticize Eurocentrism demonstrates an array of connections and conversations in and through disciplinary formations and geopolitical knowledges underlying the different manifestations of criticisms of Eurocentrism.

Chapter 5, entitled 'Constructing the Non-Western', focused on tracing the way theoretical strategies criticizing Eurocentrism entered into conversation with the disciplinary formation of International Relations. This chapter underlined that International Relations as a disciplinary formation was constructed in and through difference which allowed 'us to claim to "solve" the problem by negotiating a modus vivendi among political communities', yet the problem remained whereby 'the bounded political community constructs (and is constructed by) the other'.[13] As such, it is not just the locus of enunciation with respect to geopolitics of knowledge that needs to be underlined but also the audience and disciplinary formations being addressed. In that sense, 'It is as much the saying (and the audience involved) as what is said (and the world referred to) that preserve or transform the image of the real constructed by previous acts of saying and previous utterances'.[14] This means that criticism of Eurocentrism manifested itself in a certain way within IR because of the disciplinary formations of the field and the privileged concerns it had, and, as such, thinking in and through disciplinary formations and 'connected histories' can work to open up space that makes it possible to enter into conversation in and through disciplinary formations and geopolitical knowledges.

The aim of the book has been to underline that the story of Eurocentrism in International Relations is not one that is bounded within disciplinary formations, nor should it be told as something exclusively happening in the 'West' but rather it should be a story '*of* connections, not outside and beyond them'.[15] Section I focused on the manifestations of Eurocentrism in and through disciplines and geopolitical contexts underlining the need to think through 'connected histories' in order to trace the story of Eurocentrism. Section II focused on the criticisms of Eurocentrism in and through disciplines and geopolitical knowledges underlining the need to think through 'connected histories' in order to criticize the complex, interlinked and connected ways in which Eurocentrism manifests itself.

CONNECTING INTERNATIONAL RELATIONS

I have tried to describe my position in terms of circles, standing there in the middle. These circles contain the audiences that get to hear my story. The closest circle is the one closest to my home in Igboland, because the material I am using is their material. But unless I'm writing in the Igbo language, I use a language developed elsewhere, which is English. That affects the way I write. It even affects to some extent the stories I write. So there is, if you like, a kind of paradox there already. But then, if you can, visualize a large number of ever-widening circles, including all, like Yeats's widening gyre. As more and more people are incorporated in this network, they will get different levels of meaning out of the story, depending on what they already know, or what they suspect. These circles go on indefinitely to include, ultimately, the whole world.[16]

The aforementioned quote by Chinua Achebe (novelist and poet) summarizes the underlying concern of the book and the way forward in writing connected histories of the international and of International Relations. There are many stories of international relations as an object of inquiry and as a field of research. These stories exist within 'a large number of ever-widening circles', yet the Eurocentrism of the field has predominantly presented itself as if there is only one centre and a linear direction that expands from there. Even in the stories of Eurocentrism of International Relations the boundaries of knowledge continue to persist. The book has proposed that in order to tell the story of international relations and International Relations, 'connected histories' have to be taken into account. As Subrahmanyam argues with respect to 'connected histories', the aim should be to 'redraw maps that emerge from the problematics we wish to study rather than insert problematics to fit our pre-existing categories'.[17] In that sense, the maps of disciplines, of concepts and of theories need not be taken as bounded entities but rather the problematics that are being addressed, in this case Eurocentrism, need to be studied in and through the pregiven maps of disciplinary formations and geopolitical knowledges. As such, rethinking and re-writing through 'connected histories' enables a rethinking of 'our current circumstances and the trajectories of change associated with them from multiple perspectives, rather than a dominant European one'.[18] The tracing of manifestations of Eurocentrism and the criticisms of Eurocentrism has underlined the different trajectories and perspectives at work in attempting to criticize Eurocentrism. It is through reading and writing by connecting and relating that the classificatory archives of knowledge can be questioned.

NOTES

1. For the way in which 'connected histories' has been brought into sociology, see Bhambra, *Rethinking Modernity : Postcolonialism and the Sociological Imagination*; Bhambra, 'Historical Sociology, International Relations and Connected Histories'; *Connected Sociologies*.

2. Subrahmanyam, *Explorations in Connected Histories: From the Tagus to the Ganges*, 4.

3. 'Connected Histories: Notes Towards a Reconfiguration of Early Modern Eurasia', 761–762.

4. Sabaratnam, 'Avatars of Eurocentrism in the Critique of the Liberal Peace'.

5. Certeau, *The Writing of History*.

6. Munslow, *The New History*, 157.

7. Vaughan-Williams, 'International Relations and The problem of History'.

8. Barkawi and Laffey, 'The Postcolonial Moment in Security Studies', 334–335.

9. Trouillot, *Silencing the Past: Power and the Production of History*.

10. Berkhofer, *Beyond the Great Story: History as Text and Discourse*.

11. Buck-Morss, *Hegel, Haiti, and Universal History*.

12. Spivak, 'The Rani of Sirmur: An Essay in Reading the Archives'.

13. Inayatullah and Blaney, *International Relations and the Problem of Difference*, 6.

14. Mignolo, 'Colonial and Postcolonial Discourse: Cultural Critique or Academic Colonialism?', 128.

15. Said, *Culture and Imperialism*, 55.

16. Jerome Brooks, 'Interviews: Chinua Achebe, the Art of Fiction No. 139', http://www.theparisreview.org/interviews/1720/the-art-of-fiction-no-139-chinua-achebe.

17. Subrahmanyam, *Explorations in Connected Histories: From the Tagus to the Ganges*, 4.

18. Bhambra, *Rethinking Modernity: Postcolonialism and the Sociological Imagination*, 153.

Bibliography

Abdel-Malek, Anouar. 'Orientalism in Crisis'. *Diogenes* 11, no. 44 (1963): 103–40.

Acharya, Amitav, and Barry Buzan, eds. *Non-Western International Relations Theory: Perspectives on and Beyond Asia*. London: Routledge, 2010.

Adorno, Rolena. 'Reconsidering Colonial Discourse for Sixteenth- and Seventeenth-Century Spanish America'. *Latin American Research Review* 28, no. 3 (1993): 135–45.

Ahluwalia, Pal. 'Out of Africa: Post-Structuralism's Colonial Roots'. *Postcolonial Studies* 8, no. 2 (2005): 137–54.

Ahluwalia, Pal. *Out of Africa: Post-Structuralism's Colonial Roots*. London and New York: Routledge, 2010.

Ahmad, Aijaz. *In Theory: Classes, Nations, Literatures*. London: Verso, 1994.

Amin, Samir. *Eurocentrism*. New York: New York University Press, 1989.

Anghie, Antony. 'The Evolution of International Law: Colonial and Postcolonial Realities'. *Third World Quarterly* 27, no. 5 (2006): 739–53.

Anghie, Antony. *Imperialism, Sovereignty and the Making of International Law*. Vol. 37. Cambridge: Cambridge University Press, 2007.

Ankersmit, F. R. *Narrative Logic: A Semantic Analysis of the Historian's Language*. The Hague: M. Nijhoff, 1983.

Ankersmit, F. R. *Historical Representation*. Stanford: Stanford University Press, 2002.

Ankersmit, F. R. *Political Representation*. Stanford: Stanford University Press, 2002.

Aronna, Michael, José Oviedo, and John Beverley, eds. *The Postmodernism Debate in Latin America*. Durham and London: Duke University Press, 1995.

Ashworth, Lucian M. *A History of International Thought: From the Origins of the Modern State to Academic International Relations*. London: Routledge, 2014.

Ashworth, Lucian M. 'Did the Realist-Idealist Great Debate Really Happen? A Revisionist History of International Relations'. *International Relations* 16, no. 1 (2002): 33–51.

Ashworth, Lucian M. 'Where Are the Idealists in Interwar International Relations?'. *Review of International Studies* 32, no. 02 (2006): 291–308.

Ataöv, Türkkaya. *Nato and Turkey*. Ankara: Sevinç Print. House, 1970.

Atay, Falih Rifki. 'Decisiveness in Foreign Policy'. In *Ulus*. Ataturk IBB Kitapligi, Cilt 4, Sayi 8961–9144, 8 October 1946.

Athanassopoulou, Ekavi. *Turkey: Anglo-American Security Interests, 1945–1952: The First Enlargement of Nato*. London: Frank Cass, 1999.

Barkawi, Tarak, and Mark Laffey. 'Retrieving the Imperial: Empire and International Relations'. *Millennium-Journal of International Studies* 31, no. 1 (2002): 109–27.

Barkawi, Tarak, and Mark Laffey. 'The Postcolonial Moment in Security Studies'. *Review of International Studies* 32, no. 2 (2006): 329–52.

Bartolovich, Crystal, and Neil Lazarus. *Marxism, Modernity and Postcolonial Studies*. Cambridge: Cambridge University Press, 2002.

Bayur, Hikmet. 'America, Asia, Europe and US, Kudret, 21.08.1950'. In *Cumhuriyet Arşivi, Başbakanlık Devlet Arşivleri*. File: 408, Code: 1 204, Place: 809 1.

Bell, Duncan SA. 'International Relations: The Dawn of a Historiographical Turn?'. *The British Journal of Politics & International Relations* 3, no. 1 (2001): 115–26.

Bell, Duncan SA. 'Writing the World: Disciplinary History and Beyond'. *International Affairs* 85, no. 1 (2009): 3–22.

Bentley, Michael. *Companion to Historiography*. London: Routledge, 1997.

Berkhofer, Robert. *Beyond the Great Story: History as Text and Discourse*. Princeton, NJ: Princeton University Press, 1995.

Beverley, John, and Jose Oviedo. 'Introduction'. In *The Postmodernism Debate in Latin America*, edited by Michael Aronna and Jose Oviedo, 1–17. Durham and London: Duke University Press, 1995.

Bhabha, Homi K. *The Location of Culture*. London: Routledge, 2012.

Bhambra, Gurminder K. *Rethinking Modernity: Postcolonialism and the Sociological Imagination*. Basingstoke: Palgrave, 2007.

Bhambra, Gurminder K. 'Historical Sociology, International Relations and Connected Histories'. *Cambridge Review of International Affairs* 23, no. 1 (2010): 127–43.

Bhambra, Gurminder K. *Connected Sociologies*. London: Bloomsbury Publishing, 2014.

Bhambra, Gurminder K. 'A Sociological Dilemma: Race, Segregation and US Sociology'. *Current Sociology* 62, no. 4 (2014): 472–92.

Bilgin, Pınar. '"Only Strong States Can Survive in Turkey's Geography": The Uses of "Geopolitical Truths" in Turkey'. *Political Geography* 26, no. 7 (2007): 740–56.

Bilgin, Pınar. 'Thinking Past 'Western' IR?'. *Third World Quarterly* 29, no. 1 (2008): 5–23.

Bilgin, Pınar. 'Securing Turkey through Western-Oriented Foreign Policy'. *New Perspectives on Turkey* 45, no. 2 (2009), 105–25

Bilgin, Pınar. 'The "Western-Centrism" of Security Studies: "Blind Spot" or Constitutive Practice?'. *Security Dialogue* 41, no. 6 (2010): 615–22.

Bilgin, Pınar. 'Turkey's "Geopolitics Dogma"'. In *The Return of Geopolitics in Europe? Social Mechanisms and Foreign Policy Identity Crises*, edited by Stefano Guzzini, 151–173. Cambridge: Cambridge University Press, 2012.

Bilgin, Pınar. *The International in Security, Security in the International*. London: Routledge, 2016.

Bilgin, Pınar, and Ali Bilgiç. 'Turkey and Eu/Rope: Discourses of Inspiration/Anxiety in Turkey's Foreign Policy'. *Review of European Studies* 4, no. 3 (2012): 111.

Bilgin, Pınar, and Başak Ince. 'Security and Citizenship in the Global South: In/Securing Citizens in Early Republican Turkey (1923–1946)'. *International Relations* 29, no. 4 (2015): 500–20.

Bilgin, Pınar, and Adam David Morton. 'Historicising Representations Of "failed States": Beyond the Cold-War Annexation of the Social Sciences?'. *Third World Quarterly* 23, no. 1 (2002): 55–80.

Blaney, David L., and Arlene B. Tickner. 'Introduction: Claiming the International Beyond IR'. In *Claiming the International*, edited by David L. Blaney and Arlene B. Tickner, 1–24. London: Routledge, 2013.

Bostanoğlu, Burcu. *Türkiye-Abd İlişkilerinin Politikası: Kuram Ve Siyaset*. Ankara: İmge Kitabevi, 1999.

Bozdağlıoğlu, Yücel. *Turkish Foreign Policy and Turkish Identity: A Constructivist Approach*. London: Routledge, 2004.

Brooks, Jerome. 'Interviews: Chinua Achebe, the Art of Fiction No. 139'. http://www.theparisreview.org/interviews/1720/the-art-of-fiction-no-139-chinua-achebe.

Buck-Morss, Susan. *Hegel, Haiti, and Universal History*. Pittsburgh: University of Pittsburgh Press, 2009.

Butler, Judith. *Excitable Speech: A Politics of the Performative*. New York: Routledge, 1997.

Buzan, Barry, and Richard Little. 'World History and the Development of Non-Western International Relations Theory'. In *Non-Western International Relations Theory: Perspectives on and Beyond Asia*, edited by Amitav Acharya and Barry Buzan, 197–220. London: Routledge, 2010.

Campbell, David. 'Metabosnia: Narratives of the Bosnian War'. *Review of International Studies* 24, no. 02 (1998): 261–81.

Campbell, David. *Writing Security: United States Foreign Policy and the Politics of Identity*. Minneapolis: University of Minnesota Press, 1998.

Carr, Edward H. *What Is History*. New York: Vintage, 1967.

Certeau, Michel de. *The Writing of History*. European Perspectives. New York: Columbia University Press, 1988.

Chakrabarty, Dipesh. 'Postcoloniality and the Artifice of History: Who Speaks for "Indian" Pasts?'. *Representations*, no. 37 (1992): 1–26.

Chatterjee, Partha. *Nationalist thought and the colonial world : A derivative discourse*. London : Zed Books, 1986.

Chen, Ching-Chang. 'The Absence of Non-Western IR Theory in Asia Reconsidered'. *International Relations of the Asia-Pacific* 11, no. 1 (2011): 1–23.

Chen, Ching-Chang. 'The Im/Possibility of Building Indigenous Theories in a Hegemonic Discipline: The Case of Japanese International Relations'. *Asian Perspective* 36, no. 3 (2012): 463–92.

Clavin, Matthew J. *Toussaint Louverture and the American Civil War: The Promise and Peril of a Second Haitian Revolution*. Philadelphia: University of Pennsylvania Press, 2010.

Coş, Kıvanç, and Pınar Bilgin. 'Stalin's Demands: Constructions of the "Soviet Other" in Turkey's Foreign Policy, 1919–1945'. *Foreign Policy Analysis* 6, no. 1 (2010): 43–60.

Coulson, Andrew. *Tanzania: A Political Economy*. Oxford: Oxford University Press, 2013.

Cox, Robert W. 'Social Forces, States and World Orders: Beyond International Relations Theory'. *Millennium* 10, no. 2 (1981): 126–55.

Darby, Phillip, and Albert J. Paolini. 'Bridging International Relations and Postcolonialism'. *Alternatives: Global, Local, Political* 19, no. 3 (1994): 371–97.

Davis, Kathleen. *Periodization and Sovereignty: How Ideas of Feudalism and Secularization Govern the Politics of Time*. The Middle Ages Series. Philadelphia: University of Pennsylvania Press, 2008.

'Declaration by PM Adnan Menderes, 21.2.1951'. In *Cumhuriyet Arşivi, Başbakanlık Devlet Arşivleri*. File A6, Code: 0 30 01, Place: 13 76 7.

Deighton, Anne. 'Britain and the Cold War'. In *The Cambridge History of the Cold War, Vol.1*, edited by Melvyn P. Leffler and Odd Arne Westad, 112–32. Cambridge: Cambridge University Press, 2010.

Derian, James Der. *Antidiplomacy: Spies, Terror, Speed and War*. Cambridge: Blackwell Publishers, 1992.

Dimitrov, Vesselin. *Stalin's Cold War: Soviet Foreign Policy, Democracy and Communism in Bulgaria, 1941–48*. London: Palgrave Macmillan, 2007.

Dirlik, Arif. 'The Postcolonial Aura: Third World Criticism in the Age of Global Capitalism'. *Critical Inquiry* 20, no. 2 (1994): 328–56.

Dubois, Laurent. *Avengers of the New World*. Cambridge, MA: Harvard University Press, 2005.

Enloe, Cynthia. *The Morning After: Sexual Politics at the End of the Cold War*. Berkeley: University of California Press, 1993.

Erim, Nihat. 'The Only Missing Link, Ulus, 18 August 1946'. Atatürk IBB Kitapliği, Cilt 4, Sayı 8961–9144.

Erim, Nihat. 'Reaction to the Soviet Note, Ulus, 24 August 1946'. Atatürk IBB Kitapliği, Cilt 4, Sayı 8961–9144.

Erim, Nihat. 'With Respect to Russian Demands, Ulus, 15 August 1946'. Atatürk IBB Kitapliği, Cilt 4, Sayı 8961–9144.

Falola, Toyin. *Nationalism and African Intellectuals*. Rochester, NY: University Rochester Press, 2001.

Feis, Herbert. *From Trust to Terror: The Onset of the Cold War, 1945–1950*. New York: W.W. Norton, 1970.

Ferrer, Ada. *Freedom's Mirror*. Cambridge: Cambridge University Press, 2014.

Finney, Patrick. 'Still "Marking Time"? Text, Discourse and Truth in International History'. *Review of International Studies* 27, no. 03 (2001): 291–308.

Gaddis, John Lewis. *The United States and the Origins of the Cold War, 1941–1947*. New York: Columbia University Press, 1972.

Gaddis, John Lewis. 'The Long Peace: Elements of Stability in the Post-War International System'. *International Security* 10, no. 4 (1986): 99–142.

Gaffield, Julia. *Haitian Connections in the Atlantic World: Recognition after Revolution*. Chapel Hill, NC: UNC Press Books, 2015.

Gandhi, Leela. *Postcolonial Theory: A Critical Introduction*. New York: Columbia University Press, 1998.

Gates, Henry Louis Jr. 'Critical Fanonism'. *Critical inquiry* 17, no. 3 (1991): 457–70.

Gilbert, Bart Moore. *Postcolonial Theory*. London & New York: Verso, 1997.

Grosfoguel, Ramón. 'The Epistemic Decolonial Turn: Beyond Political-Economy Paradigms'. *Cultural Studies* 21, no. 2–3 (2007): 211–23.

Grosfoguel, Ramón. 'Decolonizing Post-Colonial Studies and Paradigms of Political Economy: Transmodernity, Decolonial Thinking, and Global Coloniality'. *Transmodernity* 1, no. 1 (2011): 1–36.

Group, Latin American Subaltern Studies. 'Founding Statement'. In *The Postmodernism Debate in Latin America*, edited by Michael Aronna, John Beverley and Jose Oviedo, 135–46. Durham and London: Duke University Press, 1995.

Grovogui, Siba. 'Regimes of Sovereignty: International Morality and the African Condition'. *European Journal of International Relations* 8, no. 3 (2002): 315–38.

Grovogui, Siba. *Sovereigns, Quasi Sovereigns, and Africans: Race and Self-Determination in International Law*. Borderlines. Minneapolis, MN: University of Minnesota Press, 1996.

Grovogui, Siba N'Zatioula. *Beyond Eurocentrism and Anarchy: Memories of International Order and Institutions*. London: Palgrave Macmillan, 2006.

Grovogui, Siba N'Zatioula. 'Mind, Body, and Gut! Elements of a Postcolonial Human Rights Discourse'. In *Decolonising International Relations*, edited by Branwyn Gruffyd Jones, 179–96. Maryland: Rowman & Littlefield, 2006.

Guha, Ranajit, ed. *Subaltern Studies, I-IV*. New Delhi: Oxford University Press, 1981–1989.

Guha, Ranajit. 'On Some Aspects of the Historiography of Colonial India'. In *Mapping Subaltern Studies and the Postcolonial*, edited by Vinayak Chaturvedi, 1–8. London: Verso Books, 2012.

Guilhot, Nicolas. 'The Realist Gambit: Postwar American Political Science and the Birth of IR Theory'. *International Political Sociology* 2, no. 4 (2008): 281–304.

Gusterson, Hugh. 'Missing the End of the Cold War in International Security'. In *Cultures of Insecurity: States, Communities and the Production of Danger*, edited by Jutta Weldes, Mark Laffey, Hugh Gusterson and Raymond Duvall, 319–46. Minneapolis: University of Minnesota Press, 1999.

Hall, Stuart. 'The West and the Rest: Discourse and Power'. In *Formations of Modernity*, edited by Stuart Hall and Bram Gieben, 275–332. New York: Cambridge Polity Press, 1992, 663–86

Hall, Stuart. 'The after-Life of Frantz Fanon: Why Fanon? Why Now? Why Black Skin, White Masks?'. In *The Fact of Blackness: Frantz Fanon and Visual Representation*, edited by Alan Read, 12–37. Seattle, WA: Bay Press, 1996.

Halle, Louis. *The Cold War as History*. London: Chatto and Windus, 1967.

Halperin, Sandra. 'International Relations Theory and the Hegemony of Western Conceptions of Modernity'. In *Decolonizing International Relations*, edited by Branwen Gruffydd Jones, 43–63. Lanham: Rowman & Littlefield, 2006.

Hamati-Ataya, Inanna. 'Worlding Beyond the Self? IR, the Subject, and the Cartesian Anxiety'. In *Claiming the International*, edited by David L. Blaney and Arlene B. Tickner, 26–43. London: Routledge, 2013.

Hammond, Andrew. 'From Rhetoric to Rollback: Introductory Thoughts on Cold War Writing'. In *Cold War Literature: Writing the Global Conflict*, edited by Andrew Hammond, 1–15. New York and London: Routledge, 2006.

Hobden, Stephen. 'Historical Sociology: Back to the Future of International Relations'. In *Historical Sociology of International Relations*, edited by Stephen Hobden and John Hobson. Cambridge: Cambridge University Press, 2002.

Hobson, John. 'Provincializing Westphalia: The Eastern Origins of Sovereignty'.
International Politics 46, no. 6 (2009): 671–90.

Hobson, John. *The Eurocentric Conception of World Politics: Western International
Theory, 1760–2010*. Cambridge: Cambridge University Press, 2012.

Hurst, Steven. *Cold War US Foreign Policy: Key Perspectives*. Edinburgh: Edinburgh University Press, 2005.

Iggers, Georg G. *Historiography in the Twentieth Century: From Scientific Objectivity to the Postmodern Challenge*. London: Wesleyan University Press, 1997.

'An Important Example, Ulus, 7 September 1946'. Ataturk Kitapliği, Cilt 4, Sayı
8961–9144.

Inayatullah, Naeem, and David L. Blaney. *International Relations and the Problem
of Difference*. London: Routledge, 2004.

Inoguchi, Takashi. 'Are There Any Theories of International Relations in Japan?'.
International Relations of the Asia-Pacific 7, no. 3 (2007): 369–90.

James, C. L. R. *The Black Jacobins*. New York: The Dial Press, 1938.

Jenkins, Keith. *On 'What Is History?'*. London: Routledge, 1995.

Jenkins, Keith. *Postmodern History Reader*. London: Routledge, 1997.

Jenkins, Keith. *Refiguring History: New Thoughts on an Old Discipline*. London:
Routledge, 2003.

Jenkins, Keith. *Rethinking History*. London: Routledge, 2003.

Jones, Branwen Gruffydd. 'Introduction: International Relations, Eurocentrism, and
Imperialism'. In *Decolonizing International Relations*, edited by Branwen Gruffydd Jones, 1–19. Lanham, MD: Rowman & Littlefield, 2006.

Keene, Edward. *Beyond the Anarchical Society: Grotius, Colonialism and Order in
World Politics*. Cambridge: Cambridge University Press, 2002.

Kipling, Rudyard. *The Collected Poems of Rudyard Kipling*. Ware: Wordsworth Editions, 1994.

Krishna, Sankaran. 'The Importance of Being Ironic: A Postcolonial View on Critical
International Relations Theory'. *Alternatives* 18, no. 3 (1993): 385–417.

Krishna, Sankaran. 'Race, Amnesia, and the Education of International Relations'.
Alternatives 26, no. 4 (2001): 401–24.

LaCapra, Dominick. *Writing History, Writing Trauma*. Baltimore: Johns Hopkins
University Press, 2001.

Laffey, Mark. 'Locating Identity: Performativity, Foreign Policy and State Action'.
Review of International Studies 26, no. 3 (2000): 429–44.

Laffey, Mark, and Jutta Weldes. 'Decolonizing the Cuban Missile Crisis'. *International Studies Quarterly* 52 (2008): 555–77.

Lawson, George. 'The Eternal Divide? History and International Relations'. *European Journal of International Relations* 18 (2010): 203–36.

Lazarus, Neil. 'What Postcolonial Theory Doesn't Say'. *Race & Class* 53, no. 1
(2011): 3–27.

Leffler, Melvyn P. *A Preponderance of Power: National Security, the Truman Administration, and the Cold War*. Stanford: Stanford University Press, 1992.

Leffler, Melvyn P. *For the Soul of Mankind: The United States, the Soviet Union, and the Cold War*. New York: Hill & Wang, 2007.

Leffler, Melvyn P. 'The Emergence of an American Grand Strategy, 1945–1952'. In *The Cambridge History of the Cold War*, edited by Melvyn P. Leffler and Odd Arne Westad. Cambridge: Cambridge University Press, 2010.

Lewis, Rupert. *Walter Rodney's Intellectual and Political Thought*. Detroit: Wayne State University Press, 1998.

Long, David, and Brian C. Schmidt. *Imperialism and Internationalism in the Discipline of International Relations*. Cambridge: Cambridge University Press, 2005.

Loomba, Ania. *Colonialism/Postcolonialism*. London: Routledge, 2015.

Loxley, James. *Performativity*. New York: Routledge, 2006.

Lugones, Maria. 'Heterosexualism and the Colonial/Modern Gender System'. *Hypatia* 22, no. 1 (2007): 186–219.

'M. Philips Price, Turkish PM's Views on the Straits Issue, Manchester Guardian, 30.11.1946'. In *Cumhuriyet Arşivi, Başbakanlık Devlet Arşivleri*. File: A6, Code: 0 30 01, Place: 11 67 3.

Maldonado-Torres, Nelson. 'On the Coloniality of Being: Contributions to the Development of a Concept'. *Cultural studies* 21, no. 2–3 (2007): 240–70.

Mallavarapu, Siddharth. 'Development of International Relations Theory in India Traditions, Contemporary Perspectives and Trajectories'. *International Studies* 46, no. 1–2 (2009): 165–83.

Mallon, Florencia E. 'The Promise and Dilemma of Subaltern Studies: Perspectives from Latin American History'. *The American Historical Review* 99, no. 5 (1994): 1491–515.

Mastny, Vojtech. *The Cold War and Soviet Insecurity: The Stalin Years*. New York: Oxford University Press, 1996.

McClintock, Anne. 'The Angel of Progress: Pitfalls of the Term "Post-Colonialism"'. *Social Text*, no. 31/32 (1992): 84–98.

McMahon, Robert J. *The Cold War on the Periphery: The United States, India, and Pakistan*. Columbia: Columbia University Press, 1994.

'Meeting with Journalists, Sükrü Saraçoğlu'. In *Cumhuriyet Arşivi, Başbakanlık Devlet Arşivleri*. File: 16, Code: 30..1.0.0, Place: 11.64.6, 5 September 1945.

Mignolo, Walter D. 'Colonial and Postcolonial Discourse: Cultural Critique or Academic Colonialism?'. *Latin American Research Review* 28, no. 3 (1993): 120–34.

Mignolo, Walter D. *Local Histories/Global Designs: Coloniality, Subaltern Knowledges, and Border Thinking*. Princeton Studies in Culture/Power/History. Princeton, NJ: Princeton University Press, 2000.

Mignolo, Walter D. 'Delinking: The Rhetoric of Modernity, the Logic of Coloniality and the Grammar of De-Coloniality 1'. *Cultural Studies* 21, no. 2–3 (2007): 449–514.

Mignolo, Walter D. *The Darker Side of Western Modernity: Global Futures, Decolonial Options*. Latin America Otherwise: Languages, Empires, Nations. Durham: Duke University Press, 2011.

Milliken, Jennifer. 'Intervention and Identity: Reconstructing the West in Korea'. In *Cultures of Insecurity: States, Communities and the Production of Danger*, edited by Jutta Weldes, Mark Laffey, Hugh Gusterson and Raymond Duvall, 91–118. Minneapolis: University of Minnesota Press, 1999.

Mishra, Vijay, and Bob Hodge. 'What Is Post (-) Colonialism?'. *Textual Practice* 5, no. 3 (1991): 399–414.

Mohanty, Chandra Talpade. 'Under Western Eyes: Feminist Scholarship and Colonial Discourses'. *Feminist Review*, no. 30 (1988): 61–88.

Mohanty, Chandra Talpade. '"Under Western Eyes" Revisited: Feminist Solidarity through Anticapitalist Struggles'. *Signs* 28, no. 2 (2003): 499–535.

Morris, Aldon. *The Scholar Denied: Web Du Bois and the Birth of Modern Sociology*. Berkeley: University of California Press, 2015.

Morrison, Toni. 'Unspeakable Things Unspoken: The Afro-American Presence in American Literature'. *Michigan Quarterly Review* 28, no. Winter (1989): 1–34.

Munslow, Alun. *Deconstructing History*. London; New York: Routledge, 1997.

Munslow, Alun. *The New History*. London: Routledge, 2003.

Muppidi, Himadeep. *Politics in Emotion: The Song of Telangana*. New York: Routledge, 2014.

Narayan, Uma. 'Essence of Culture and a Sense of History: A Feminist Critique of Cultural Essentialism'. *Hypatia* 13, no. 2 (1998): 86–106.

Nayak, Meghana, and Eric Selbin. *Decentering International Relations*. London; New York: Zed, 2010.

'New York Times Correspondent on Turkey'. In *Cumhuriyet Arşivi, Başbakanlık Devlet Arşivleri*. File: A6, Code: 30..1.0.0, Place:12.70.5., 17 April 1947.

'Nihat Erim Kocaeli Speech (the Changing of the Press Law)'. In *Cumhuriyet Arşivi, Başbakanlık Devlet Arşivleri*. File: A6, Code: 30..1.0.0, Place:11.65.7.

'Nihat Erim, "in the Face of a Complicated Nature," Ulus, 1 December 1948'. In *Cumhuriyet Arşivi, Başbakanlık Devlet Arşivleri*. File: A6, Code: 30..1.0.0, Place: 11.68.6.

'Nihat Erim, in the Face of a Complicated Picture, Ulus Newspaper, 1 December 1948'. In *Cumhuriyet Arşivi, Başbakanlık Devlet Arşivleri*. File: A6, Code: 0 30 01, Place: 11 68 2, 1 December 1948.

Onslow, Sue. *Cold War in Southern Africa: White Power, Black Liberation*. London and New York: Routledge, 2009.

Pahuja, Sundhya. *Decolonising International Law: Development, Economic Growth and the Politics of Universality*. Vol. 86. Cambridge: Cambridge University Press, 2011.

'Parliament Meeting, 28.5.1947'. In *Cumhuriyet Arşivi, Başbakanlık Devlet Arşivleri*. File: A6, Code: 30 01, Place: 12 71 3.

Parry, Benita. *Postcolonial Studies: A Materialist Critique*. London/New York: Routledge, 2004.

Prakash, Gyan. 'Orientalism Now'. *History and Theory* 34 (1995): 199–212.

'Prime Minister's Speech, 6.4.1946'. In *Cumhuriyet Arşivi, Başbakanlık Devlet Arşivleri*. File:A6, Code: 0 30 01, Place: 11 65 2.

'Questions Submitted to H.E. M. Adnan Menderes, Prima Minister of Turkey, by Mr. Ralph Izzard, Special Correspondent to the Daily Mail, London, 5 June 1950'. In *Cumhuriyet Arşivi, Başbakanlık Devlet Arşivleri*. File: E4, Code: 30..1.0.0, Place:60.372..2.

Quijano, Anibal. 'Modernity, Identity, and Utopia in Latin America'. In *The Postmodernism Debate in Latin America*, edited by Michael Aronna, John

Beverley and Jose Oviedo, 201–16. Durham and London: Duke University Press, 1995.

Quijano, Aníbal. 'Coloniality and Modernity/Rationality'. *Cultural studies* 21, no. 2–3 (2007): 168–78.

Quirk, Joel, and Darshan Vigneswaran. 'The Construction of an Edifice: The Story of a First Great Debate'. *Review of International Studies* 31, no. 1 (2005): 89–107.

Raj, Kapil. 'Beyond Postcolonialism … and Postpositivism: Circulation and the Global History of Science'. *Isis* 104, no. 2 (2013): 337–47.

Ranger, Terence. 'Subaltern Studies and "Social History"'. *Southern African Review of Books* 3 (1990): 3–4.

Rao, Rahul. 'Recovering Reparative Readings of Postcolonialism and Marxism'. *Critical Sociology* (2016): 0896920516630798.

Rigney, Ann. *The Rhetoric of Historical Representation: Three Narrative Histories of the French Revolution*. Cambridge: Cambridge University Press, 2002.

Robinson, Cedric J. *Black Marxism: The Making of the Black Radical Tradition*. Chapel Hill, NC: University of North Carolina Press, 1983.

Robinson, Cedric. 'The Appropriation of Frantz Fanon'. *Race & Class* 35, no.1 (1993): 79–91.

Rodney, Walter. *How Europe Underdeveloped Africa*. Washington: Howard University Press, 1974.

Rosenberg, Emily. 'Considering Borders'. In *Explaining the History of American Foreign Relations*, edited by M. J. Hogan and T. G. Paterson, 188–202. Cambridge: Cambridge University Press, 2004.

Sabaratnam, Meera. 'Avatars of Eurocentrism in the Critique of the Liberal Peace'. *Security Dialogue* 44, no. 3 (2013): 259–78.

Sadak, Necmettin. 'Atlantic Pact and Turkey, Aksam, 15.08.1950'. In *Cumhuriyet Arşivi, Başbakanlık Devlet Arşivleri*. File: 408, Code: 1 204, Place: 809 1.

Said, Edward W.. *Orientalism*. New York: Vitage Books, 1978.

Said, Edward W. *The World, the Text, and the Critic*. Cambridge, MA: Harvard University Press, 1983.

Said, Edward W. 'Orientalism Reconsidered'. *Cultural Critique*, no. 1 (1985): 89–107.

Said, Edward W. *Culture and Imperialism*. New York: Vintage Books, 1994.

Sajed, Alina. *Postcolonial Encounters in International Relations: The Politics of Transgression in the Maghreb*. London: Routledge, 2013.

Saull, Richard. 'Locating the Global South in the Theorisation of the Cold War: Capitalist Development, Social Revolution and Geopolitical Conflict'. *Third World Quarterly* 26, no. March (2005): 253–80.

Schmidt, Brian C. *The Political Discourse of Anarchy: A Disciplinary History of International Relations*. Albany: SUNY Press, 1998.

Schmidt, Brian C., ed. *International Relations and the First Great Debate*: London and New York: Routledge, 2013.

Scott, David. 'The Social Construction of Postcolonial Studies'. In *Postcolonial Studies and Beyond*, edited by Ania Looma, Suvir Kaul, Matti Bunzl, Antoinette Burton and Jed Esty, 385–400. Durham, NC: Duke University Press, 2005.

Seed, Patricia. 'Colonial and Postcolonial Discourse'. *Latin American Research Review* 26, no. 3 (1991): 181–200.

Seed, Patricia. 'More Colonial and Postcolonial Discourses'. *Latin American Research Review* 28, no. 3 (1993): 146–52.

Sertel, Zekeriya. *Hatirladıklarım*. Istanbul: Remzi Kitabevi, 1977.

Seth, Sanjay. 'Postcolonial Theory and the Critique of International Relations'. *Millennium-Journal of International Studies* 40, no. 1 (2011): 167–83.

Sever, Aysegul. 'Soguk Savas Kusatmasinda Turkiye, Bati Ve Orta Dogu 1945–1958'. Istanbul: Boyut Kitaplari, 1997.

Shilliam, Robbie. 'What About Marcus Garvey? Race and the Transformation of Sovereignty Debate'. *Review of International Studies* 32, no. 3 (2006): 379–400.

Shilliam, Robbie, ed. *International Relations and Non-Western Thought: Imperialism, Colonialism and Investigations of Global Modernity*. London: Routledge, 2010.

Shilliam, Robbie. 'The Perilous but Unavoidable Terrain of the Non-West'. In *International Relations and Non-Western Thought: Imperialism, Colonialism and Investigations of Global Modernity*, edited by Robbie Shilliam, 12–25. London: Routledge, 2010.

Shilliam, Robbie. 'Civilization and the Poetics of Slavery'. *Thesis Eleven* 108, no. 1 (2012): 99–117.

Shilliam, Robbie. 'Intervention and Colonial-Modernity: Decolonising the Italy/Ethiopia Conflict through Psalms 68: 31'. *Review of International Studies* 39, no. 5 (2013): 1131–47.

Shilliam, Robbie. '"Open the Gates Mek We Repatriate": Caribbean Slavery, Constructivism, and Hermeneutic Tensions'. *International Theory* 6, no. 2 (2014): 349–72.

Shilliam, Robbie. 'What the Haitian Revolution Might Tell Us About Development, Security, and the Politics of Race'. *Comparative Studies in Society and History* 50, no. 3 (2008): 778–808.

Shimizu, Kosuke. 'Materializing the "Non-Western": Two Stories of Japanese Philosophers on Culture and Politics in the Inter-War Period'. *Cambridge Review of International Affairs* 28, no. 1 (2015): 3–20.

Shohat, Ella. 'Notes on the "Post-Colonial"'. *Social Text*, no. 31/32 (1992): 99–113.

Shohat, Ella, and Robert Stam. *Unthinking Eurocentrism: Multiculturalism and the Media*. London and New York: Routledge, 2014.

Simavi, Sedat. 'American Aid, Hurriyet, 14 January 1951'. In *Cumhuriyet Arşivi, Başbakanlık Devlet Arşivleri*. File: 1. BURO, Code:490..1.0.0, Place:204.811.3.

Spivak, Gayatri Chakravorty. 'The Rani of Sirmur: An Essay in Reading the Archives'. *History and Theory* 24, no. 3 (1985): 247–72.

Spivak, Gayatri Chakravorty. 'Three Women's Texts and a Critique of Imperialism'. *Critical inquiry* 12, no. 1 (1985): 243–61.

Stam, Robert, and Ella Shohat. 'French Intellectuals and the Postcolonial'. *Interventions* 14, no. 1 (2012): 83–119.

Subrahmanyam, Sanjay. 'Connected Histories: Notes Towards a Reconfiguration of Early Modern Eurasia'. *Modern Asian Studies* 31, no. 3 (1997): 735–62.

Subrahmanyam, Sanjay. *Explorations in Connected Histories: From the Tagus to the Ganges*. Oxford: Oxford University Press, 2005.

Suleri, Sara. 'Woman Skin Deep: Feminism and the Postcolonial Condition'. *Critical inquiry* 18, no. 4 (1992): 756–69.

Suzuki, Shogo. *Civilization and Empire: China and Japan's Encounter with European International Society*. London: Routledge, 2009.

Tekeli, Esat. 'America's Independence Day'. In *Ulus*. Ataturk IBB Kitapligi, Cilt 4, Sayi 8961–9144, 6 July 1945.

Tibawi, A. L. *English-Speaking Orientalists: A Critique of Their Approach to Islam and Arab Nationalism*. Geneva: Islamic Centre, 1965.

Tickner, Arlene B. 'By Way of Conclusion: Forget IR?'. In *Claiming the International*, edited by David L. Blaney and Arlene B.Tickner, 214–31. London: Routledge, 2013.

Tickner, Arlene B., and David L. Blaney, eds. *Claiming the International*. London: Routledge, 2013.

Tickner, Arlene B., and David L. Blaney, eds. *Thinking International Relations Differently*: London and New York: Routledge, 2013.

Tickner, Arlene B., and Ole Wæver, eds. *International Relations Scholarship around the World*. London: Routledge, 2009.

Tickner, Ole Waever and Arlene B. 'Introduction: Geocultural Epistemologies'. In *International Relations Scholarship around the World*, edited by Ole Waever and Arlene B. Tickner, 1–31. London: Routledge, 2009.

Trouillot, Michel-Rolph. *Silencing the Past: Power and the Production of History*. Boston: Beacon Press, 1995.

Tsygankov, Andrei P., and Pavel A Tsygankov. 'National Ideology and IR Theory: Three Incarnations of The "Russian Idea"'. *European Journal of International Relations* (2010).

Varadharajan, Asha. *Exotic Parodies: Subjectivity in Adorno, Said, and Spivak*. Minneapolis, MN: University of Minnesota Press, 1995.

Vaughan-Williams, Nick. 'International Relations and the "problem of History"'. *Millennium-Journal of International Studies* 34, no. 1 (2005): 115–36.

Veric, Charlie Samuya. 'Third World Project, or How Poco Failed'. *Social Text* 31, no. 1 114 (2013): 1–20.

Vidal, Hernan. 'The Concept of Colonial and Postcolonial Discourse: A Perspective from Literary Criticism'. *Latin American Research Review* 28, no. 3 (1993): 113–19.

Vitalis, Robert. 'The Noble American Science of Imperial Relations and Its Laws of Race Development'. *Comparative Studies in Society and History* 52, no. 4 (2010): 909–38.

Vitalis, Robert. *White World Order, Black Power Politics: The Birth of American International Relations*. Ithaca, New York: Cornell University Press, 2015.

Waever, Ole. 'The Rise and Fall of the Inter-Paradigm Debate'. In *International Theory: Positivism and Beyond*, edited by Ken Booth and Marysia Zalewski Steve Smith, 149–85. Cambridge: Cambridge University Press, 1996.

Walker, Rob B. J. 'History and Structure in the Theory of International Relations'. *Millennium-Journal of International Studies* 18, no. 2 (1989): 163–83.

Wallerstein, Immanuel. 'Eurocentrism and Its Avatars: The Dilemmas of Social Science'. *Sociological bulletin* 46, no. 1 (1997): 21–39.

Weber, Cynthia. 'Performative States'. *Millennium-Journal of International Studies* 27, no. 1 (1998): 77–95.

Weldes, Jutta, Mark Laffey, Hugh Gusterson, and Raymond Duvall, eds. *Cultures of Insecurity: States, Communities and the Production of Danger*. Minneapolis: University of Minnesota Press, 1999.

Westad, Odd Arne. *The Global Cold War: Third World Interventions and the Making of Our Times*. Cambridge: Cambridge University Press, 2005.

White, Hayden. *Metahistory: The Historical Imagination in Nineteenth-Century Europe*. Baltimore and London: Johns Hopkins University, 1973.

White, Hayden. *Tropics of Discourse: Essays in Cultural Criticism*. Baltimore: John Hopkins University Press, 1978.

White, Hayden. *The Content of the Form: Narrative Discourse and Historical Representation*. Baltimore: John Hopkins University Press, 2009.

Williams, William Appelman. *The Tragedy of American Diplomacy*. New York: Delta, 1962.

Yaqing, Qin. 'Why Is There No Chinese International Relations Theory?'. *International Relations of the Asia-Pacific* 7, no. 3 (2007): 313–40.

'Yeni Sabah, Newspaper Clippings, 8 August 1950'. In *Cumhuriyet Arşivi, Başbakanlık Devlet Arşivleri*. File: 1. BURO, Code:490..1.0.0, Place:204.811.3.

Yılmaz, Eylem, and Pınar Bilgin. 'Constructing Turkey's "Western" Identity During the Cold War: Discourses of the Intellectuals of Statecraft'. *International Journal* 61, no. 1 (2005): 39–59.

'You Can Not Threaten the Existence of the Turkish Nation, Ulus, 18 December 1946'. Ataturk Kitapliği, Cilt 4, Sayı 8961–9144.

Young, Robert. *Postcolonialism: An Historical Introduction*. Oxford: Blackwell, 2001.

Young, Robert J. C. *White Mythologies: Writing History and the West*. Florence, KY: Psychology Press, 2004.

Young, Robert J. C. *Colonial Desire: Hybridity in Theory, Culture and Race*. Routledge, 2005.

Zarakol, Ayşe. *After Defeat: How the East Learned to Live with the West*. Cambridge: Cambridge University Press, 2010.

'Zekeriya Sertel's Letter, 24 April 1951'. *Cumhuriyet Arşivi, Başbakanlık Devlet Arşivleri*: File: B2, Code: 30..1.0.0, Place: 41.243..9.

Index

About the Author

Zeynep Gülşah Çapan is Visiting Lecturer at the University Erfurt, Germany. She has published articles and book chapters on the relationship between history and international relations and on Eurocentrism in International Relations.

CPSIA information can be obtained at www.ICGtesting.com
Printed in the USA
BVOW08*0951090916

461326BV00006B/2/P